Funds for this Book were Donated by:

Chapter 15 North Bay Counties
INTERNATIONAL FOOTPRINT ASSOCIATION

I.F.A. is a social association established
in 1929 to promote respect, fellowship and
mutual understanding between law enforcement officers and civilians.

Police Operations

Police
Operations

HV
7921
. P34

Gwynne Peirson
Howard University, Washington, D.C.

 Nelson-Hall Law Enforcement Series
George W. O'Connor, *Consulting Editor*
Superintendent of Public Safety, Troy, New York

Nelson-Hall / Chicago

Library of Congress Cataloging in Publication Data

Peirson, Gwynne.
  Poliee operations.

  (Nelson-Hall law enforcement series)
  Bibliography: p.
  Includes index.
  1. Police. I. Title.
HV7921.P34   363.2   75-44334
ISBN 0-911012-86-9

Manufactured in the United States of America

Contents

CHAPTER 1

The Demand for Competence

There is an increasing recognition throughout this country that successful law enforcement by police requires not only scientific technology but also a sociological approach to the understanding of people's problems and the underlying reasons for criminality. Furthermore, many persons in the law enforcement field have come to believe that a police department today must accept a role as the most active social service agency in the community.

Although the ability to call on large numbers of heavily-armed police officers is still a necessity in certain situations in many cities, police work on the whole has become much more than the ability to put down violence with a show of force. More important is the ability of police officers to understand their role in helping the community in which they work and in recognizing the many social crises that may be at the bottom of a multitude of problems with which they will be called upon to deal. This is not to say that officers will not be called upon, or need to know how, to protect themselves or others against physical violence. The present problem is that the police department's service to the community no longer ends with the suppression of violence or the arrest of a criminal offender. It is becoming increasingly more common for a majority of calls for police services to be noncriminal in nature. Despite expressions of resentment against lawful authority, citizens are becoming more prone to turn to the police for assistance in solving problems that are not basically criminal.

A study by the President's Commission on Law Enforcement and Administration of Justice pointed out that the police throughout the country constitute approximately 420,000 sworn personnel, representing more than 40,000 separate law enforcement agencies, and that these agencies spend a total of more than 2.5 billion dollars a year.[1] When one recognizes that for all practical purposes the police, who represent the induction phase of the criminal justice system, are the only phase of the system that operates fully staffed twenty-four hours a day and seven days a week, one can see that the functions of the other segments of the system depend largely on the quality of the police.

The amount of discretion that the police officer must exercise is enormous. The awareness by the individual officer of the discretionary alternatives available to him in the performance of his duties, along with a thorough understanding of his legal duties and their limitations, is reflected by both the respect he receives within the community he serves and the respect with which his opinions and actions are received by other persons in the law enforcement field.

Police Training

Throughout the United States, observers of police departments recognize the need for increasing the educational level of all police officers and for raising the educational requirements of all police applicants. The President's Commission pointed out that ". . . police today are confronted with some of the most perplexing social and behavioral problems we have ever known"[2] and that therefore it is vital to equip these officers to perform highly complex and sensitive functions.

Existing police training programs are better than no training at all, but generally they are still minimal in scope and inadequate in that for the most part they are not taught by qualified instructors. Most departments designate certain officers as "training officers" and assign them the responsibility for training with little regard for any real ability or training an officer might—or might not—have. While officers assigned to such duties may be well versed in the mechanics of police operations, new officers need a solid foundation in the principles of politics and government and basic sociology—areas of study in which the average police officer is not competent to instruct.

Some states have established commissions that have set minimum acceptable standards of training for police officers. Two of the most extensive training programs that have evolved from such commissions are in New York and California. Under the New York program, all recruits must satisfactorily complete a training program of 240 hours before they are qualified to serve as police officers in that state. California's plan, by comparison, is voluntary in that the Commission on Peace Officer Standards and Training (POST) has set minimum standards for training and is authorized to reimburse all qualified jurisdictions for up to half of the necessary living expenses of all officers who undergo the training course away from home. Under the California plan, recruits must have a minimum of 200 hours of prescribed training before a department can qualify for state aid.

Many small departments, however, have neither the time, the finances, nor sufficient personnel to allow them to relieve some of their officers from duty for training periods ranging from a few weeks to a month. The lack of training available to officers from small communities can adversely affect an officer's career in several ways. Aside from the obvious promotional advantages of advanced training, certain recommended concepts for future law enforcement would definitely work to the disadvantage of an untrained or undertrained officer if and when they are put into practice.

Studies have concluded that in order to reduce or eliminate duplication of police services, decrease delays in service, and increase the quality of law enforcement in a large metropolitan area, the many separate police departments in such an area should be unified into one metropolitan police agency.[3] If such consolidation takes place, officers from smaller departments, with little or no formal law enforcement training, would be at a definite disadvantage when forced to compete for promotion with—or even to work with—officers who have had the advantage of several hundred hours in a specialized training program.

Similar studies, conducted by the California Commission on Peace Officer Standards and Training, have recommended that all departments within the state that meet the Commission's standards have an arrangement whereby lateral entry be a part of the department's hiring practice. Under this system, an officer holding the rank of sergeant in one department would be eligible for transfer to another department that had a vacancy at that rank. This practice, which would involve only departments meeting the POST training standards, would afford individual officers the opportunity to apply for transfer to other departments in which they feel they might have better advancement possibilities. Likewise, officers with specialized training from large departments could conceivably be interested in moving to a smaller department where their training background would put them in an advantageous position for advancement.

The degree to which educational achievement has been stressed in police departments over the past several years can be seen in comparisons from statistics of a 1966 study to similar statistics for 1971. The 1966 survey of police officers in the metropolitan Detroit area showed that of 5,700 officers, over 75 percent had not attended college, and nearly 13 percent of that number had not graduated from high school. These figures compared favorably at that time with the level of educational achievement for police officers throughout the country.

By comparison, a 1971 survey published by the California Bureau of Criminal Statistics showed that of 36,641 sworn police officers within the state, 16,340 had some college background. Additionally, 5,543 had received an A.A. degree, and another 2,076 had received a B.A. degree. Another 183 had received a graduate degree.[4] These figures indicate that nearly two-thirds of all California police officers had received some college training, and more than 20 percent of the more than 36,000 officers had received a college degree.

One of the aims of this text is to fill what might otherwise be an educational void for officers from smaller departments. Over the past several years, the drive toward professionalism in police law enforcement has primarily focused on the role of the officers in middle-sized or large departments. Most large departments have separate units that specialize in traffic enforcement, vice control, community relations, juvenile problems, intelligence, and so on. To a degree, the officer in a larger department is therefore trained to be a specialist. The officer in a smaller department, on the other hand, is usually expected to be proficient in *all* these areas, and to function in them as a regular part of his patrol duties. As opposed to being a specialist, he has more need to be a generalist with sufficient knowledge and experience to allow him to function with competence in any particular situation in which he may find himself.

A practical example of one of the most common differences in the expertise expected from officers in large and small departments is the manner in which criminal investigations, particularly homicides and burglaries, are handled. A large department not only has officers specifically assigned to duty as criminal investigators or detectives, but within that area of specialization each investigator usually handles only one specific type of offense, such as robbery, burglary, forgery, and so forth.

In a large department a patrol officer who is assigned to a homicide or a burglary is only expected to institute a preliminary investigation while awaiting the arrival of more experienced officers to take over the investigation. In many departments he is specifically forbidden to take any actions that would be classified as part of an active investigation. He is expected to determine what crime was committed, call for whatever specialists are indicated (doctor, coroner, detective, and so on), and protect the crime scene while awaiting the arrival of the specialists.

Most small departments need patrol officers with the ability to make judgments and take action that will result in criminal investigation that will stand up in court. The small department patrol officer is often called upon to discover the crime, report it, investigate it, recover and preserve evidence, take statements, interrogate witnesses and suspects, and then present his findings in court in a competent manner. With the increasing pressures placed on the police by the rising crime rate, it is often impractical for a department to hire a police officer and then take months to train him to the necessary degree of competence. Therefore, departments are looking more and more for officers who either already have education or training in the criminal justice field or who exhibit the desire and drive to obtain the education on their own.

It is the author's belief that although the officer has decided to study on his own, merely reading a text is not sufficient to stimulate or challenge him to relate the text to his own experiences or opinions. For that reason this book includes a further element in the training process in the form of suggested supplementary readings at the end of many chapters. These readings have been selected to furnish a basis for relating training material to situations and problems as they have been viewed by both those who have studied law enforcement problems from a theoretical or sociological perspective and those who have had actual experience in dealing with these problems. These readings will range from a chapter to several chapters of another book. There seems no need to suggest entire books for outside reading, although a few books, such as *The New Centurions*, will probably prove so interesting to the reader that they will be read in their entirety.

The intent of suggesting these readings is not so much to encourage the reader to agree with the various texts as it is to make him aware of the problems and how they are viewed by different persons who are recognized as being knowledgeable in the field. The reader is encouraged to evaluate the various positions or theories and to recognize the rationale behind them.

To be a successful professional law enforcement officer, an individual must do more than merely apply the law and carry out the written duties of his position. He must, as in every other profession, familiarize himself with the problems and their underlying causes. Additionally, he must be familiar with research, advancements, and all current literature pertaining to the field.

Necessary Qualities for an Officer

Before discussing the skills and knowledge necessary for being an efficient and professional police officer, let us consider the kind of person best suited for the position. All the skills and knowledge of the profession cannot make *any* man a good police officer. It takes a certain kind of man with a certain kind of character to fulfill the vast array of duties assigned to the policeman. In the early part of the century August Volmer, former Berkeley Police Chief, observed:

> The first step in any plan to make our police departments more competent to control crime is keeping out, rather than removal after they get in, of undesirable, incompetent, and physically or mentally unfit persons from the police force. An unfit or incompetent policeman weakens the moral fiber of his associates and at the same time destroys the confidence of the public in the department. The protective organization suffers, and society always pays the bill when the policemen of a community are dishonest, brutal, stupid, and physically or temperamentally unsuited to their work.[5]

This statement, because of increased police responsibilities, is even more true today. Increasing reference in literature to police as the only twenty-four-hour-a-day social agency illustrates the changing and more demanding role of the police officer. The position of peace officer involves more than arresting violators; it requires an array of sociological skills that can assist in promoting peace and tranquillity in the community. The modern policeman more than ever needs the proper mental, physical and temperamental attributes in addition to a sufficient educational background.

The question then arises of how to find out whether or not an individual has the proper attributes. There is no sure-fire method of preservice evaluation. No matter what method of judging is applied, a few "bad apples" will wind up in the barrel. It is imperative, however, that every training program have certain methods of evaluating potential personnel on a psychological basis. Even in small departments it is often possible to include in the training program role-playing situations during which new officers can be evaluated as to temperament, judgment, maturity, and reaction under stress. If an officer is placed in a position where he is subject to verbal abuse and where his authority is challenged, it is important to observe whether he resorts to physical force as a means of enforcing respect for himself, or whether he handles himself in a way that will be most likely to help him enforce the law while de-escalating the potential for violence. Similarly, it is important to observe whether the officer's reactions toward a citizen or a suspect are affected by the person's ethnic background or social class. An officer who uses his official position to act out his personal prejudices is a potential source of danger to himself and his department.

In instances where there is no in-service training for officers and where individuals, whether they be working officers or applicants for the position, are studying on their own, it is for the individual's own good—and in some cases for his own safety—that he attempt to evaluate his personality in regard to the demands made on him by the job. An officer who believes that he may not be suited for the job, but who attempts to keep it as a means of employment, is doing himself a disservice. Aside from the great emotional strain that can be placed on a police officer, he can be asked to make split-second decisions that can affect his entire future.

Trite as it may sound, the fundamental requirement for being a good police officer is the ability to observe and learn. Police work is not suitable for the fearful or fainthearted, just as it is not the job for someone who feels that most disagreements are best settled by force or violence. It is not to be expected that the new recruit will enter the job with all the knowledge, skills, and attitudes that are necessary for becoming a successful law enforcement officer. What is necessary is that he enter without prejudices and biases that will impair his ability to deal rationally and evenhandedly with the problems and situations with which he will be faced.

For the police to gain greater acceptance and more respect for their role from all segments of society, it will be necessary for them to have a greater degree of preparation for a job that is becoming increasingly complicated. The amount of advance training that the average individual gets prior to taking on the duties of a police officer is minimal. One study indicated that in the occupation of physician, embalmer, barber, and beautician, the average number of training hours required before the individual was allowed to practice the occupation was 5,300. By contrast, the average preservice training for a police officer is less than 200 hours.[6]

To many potential applicants for police work, training consists primarily of physical exercises and marksmanship training with pistols and rifles. Police work is not only physical effort, however. Perhaps more important is the ability to get along with people, generally called the ability to communicate, and repeated refresher courses—either formal or informal—whereby the officer keeps himself abreast of changes in the laws and the latest interpretations of these laws.

The area that some administrators view as the most crucial is an officer's ability to gain credibility with and respect from both his coworkers and citizens in the community. Veteran officers are well aware that their most useful tool in investigating criminal offenses, or in merely gaining information about what is going on in their area of patrol, is the respect and cooperation of the citizenry. It is not at all unusual for a respected officer to receive the assistance and cooperation of the so-called criminal element on his beat, as well as that of the businessman or homeowner.

In one sense, the officer's personality and his training background are more important in a smaller department where the actions and attitudes of an individual officer more closely affect the overall reputation of his department than would be the case in a larger one. A police officer who can maintain his "cool" and let his good judgment, training, and discipline determine his actions rather than being motivated by temper, prejudice, or fear, is well on his way to becoming a leader within his profession.

Patrol

There are two basic theories of patrol. One is to patrol in such a way as to attract attention to the officer's presence. This is preventative patrol, and the underlying theory is that the presence of an officer acts as a deterrent to anyone contemplating crime. The fact that police officers are distinctively uniformed—and in some cities ride in cars that are easily recognizable—is basic to this theory.

The other theory of patrol is based on the officer's blending in with the area he is patrolling so as to attract as little attention to his presence as possible. In this practice the officer makes a point of not following a predetermined schedule and of attempting to observe the actions of the public without their being aware of his presence, or at least not being aware that he is observing them.

The role of the beat patrol officer varies according to whether he is on foot or in a car. Foot patrol officers have more freedom to institute contacts with citizens and potential suspects, while the officer assigned to a car is restricted in his citizen contacts by the control that is exercised over his movements by the police radio system.

One primary advantage of foot patrol is that the presence of an officer throughout the day or night gives a greater sense of security to citizens in the area than does the more impersonal presence of a patrol car. Over the past ten years many departments have begun phasing out foot patrol units, only to find, particularly in business areas, that people resent the absence of the officer on the beat who drops into the place of business several times a day. People generally want to know the officer on their beat. They feel safer if an officer comes by periodically. And the mere presence of the officer tends to discourage illegal activities that might otherwise have taken place. If a potential shoplifter knows that a beat officer is likely to drop into a store at any time, he usually decides that trying to steal anything there is too risky. In addition, potential thieves often feel that any officer who sees them, even when they are engaged in some innocent activity, is likely to remember them if a crime is later committed at the same location.

One of the major disadvantages of foot patrol is that the officer is less mobile and less available for radio assignment than is the officer in a car. Basically, the role of the foot patrol officer is one of prevention before the criminal act, while the car beat officer is more effective in apprehending the offender after the fact. Radio cars are involved in preventive patrol, but on a more impersonal basis. An officer assigned to a radio car on beat patrol is likely to look for suspicious-looking cars rather than suspicious-looking persons. This includes parked cars as well as those being driven, for an experienced officer knows that certain types of cars do not fit the locality, or that cars are not ordinarily parked at some locations late at night or in the early morning hours. Such an officer will check suspiciously parked cars periodically during his tour of duty, and will probably make an early check to determine whether the car has been listed as stolen or is registered in some other locality or state.

Whether an officer is assigned to foot or car patrol, it will probably be to his advantage to incorporate elements of both theories of patrol into his method of operation. That is, in some instances he will make himself visible as a means of preventative patrol, and at other times he will place himself so that he can observe while his own presence goes unnoticed. In some instances it will even be to the officer's advantage to be able to observe the actions of groups or individuals both before and after they become aware of his presence. A change in the actions or attitudes of such persons can often be a good tipoff to the officer that something is developing that needs his further attention. This type of patrol and observation develops into something like a cat-and-mouse game in which the officer, by giving the impression that he is unaware of anything unusual, can at times lull the persons in whom he is interested into taking some action that will give him a further clue to their intentions.

The officer working a beat, whether it be a walking beat or a car beat, must possess certain information that is essential to doing his job and to assuring his personal protection. This type of information is sometimes termed "street knowledge" and involves a thorough geographic knowledge of the area in which he is working and an equally thorough knowledge of the residents of the area. An officer should attempt to gain "street knowledge" as quickly as possible once he has been assigned to a beat, for it is outside the area of training that he would receive in a classroom.

Unfortunately, this type of knowledge can be gained only by experience and by the officer's recognition that each day on the force should be a part of a continuing learning process. This is not to say, however, that the necessary knowledge can only be gained by personal experience. Second-hand experience can be gained by talking with experienced officers, by reading reports submitted by other officers, and by reading books dealing with police work.

Years ago, most police officers had grown up in the community in which they were employed, and they therefore had the advantage of many years of familiarity with the area. Today, however, more and more police officers are new to the area in which they are employed. In some cases they have little or no knowledge of the city, much less of the back alleys, the streets or alleys that can be reached by going through back doors of business places, or the buildings that have common or connecting roofs.

It is no exaggeration that in some cases such knowledge—or the lack of it—can be the difference between life and death for an officer. Additionally, if an officer knows the location of all entrances and exits to an area, he greatly increases the chances that he will be able to apprehend suspects attempting to flee.

At times an officer needs immediate assistance, whether it be for his personal protection or for assistance in the prevention of a crime. When calling for help on the police radio he does not have time to look for the nearest street sign in order to inform the radio dispatcher of his location. It is absolutely necessary for an officer to know his location at all times. He should know whether the street he is on runs north and south or east and west and what hundred block he is in. While many times it is difficult to spot an exact address, an officer should be able to tell the dispatcher whether the location in question is on the even- or odd-numbered side of the street. This is a seemingly minor point, but it is surprising that many people are unaware that odd-numbered addresses are on one side of the street and even numbers on the other.

Detailed knowledge of an area can be of assistance to an officer in other ways too. For example, in questioning a suspect, an officer's knowledge of which businesses are open or closed can often assist him in tripping the suspect up in his story.

In addition to knowing street and business locations, the police officer should know the location of hospitals, schools, parks, rest homes and all-night drugstores. Knowledge of the locations of schools and parks can help an officer who has received a report of a missing child or a suspected child molester. Many small children tend to follow older children to such locations, and these, along with public restrooms, are a natural "hunting ground" for persons who might prey on children. The knowledge of the location of rest homes in his patrol area can assist an officer who finds elderly or senile persons wandering about the streets. On occasions such persons are allowed to take short walks away from the rest home and sometimes become confused or forgetful from fatigue or fright. The reason the police officer should know the locations of all-night drugstores is that one of the more commonly performed public services that an officer working a late night shift is called upon to perform is directing a citizen to such a store.

Naturally, an officer should know the locations of all pay phones and police call boxes. The police radio is inappropriate for certain communication, and the officer will have to rely on telephone communication to pass on information quickly.

While it is true that some departments are still oriented toward grid, or planned, patrol, this system is less effective in dealing with the problems faced by most beat patrol officers. In grid patrol the officer usually covers his beat by first walking down all the streets that run in the same general direction, and then patrolling the streets that run in the opposite direction. While this method assures that the officer will cover the entire assigned area within his watch period, it is more compatible with the watchman method of patrol in which the officer's primary role is to check on places of business. This method of patrol does not give special attention to areas that may be more attractive to a criminal element, nor does it allow for concentration on areas where large numbers of persons gather at particular hours.

Some methods of patrol that were instituted many years ago for a particular reason are still in use today even though they are no longer effective. One such practice is requiring officers to call in to their station at a predetermined time on the police call box. Before the widespread use of police radios, this practice served a definite purpose. These phone calls were sometimes referred to as "making a mark," and they told an officer's superior when and where the officer could be contacted. They also allowed the superior to check on the officer's well-being. If an officer did not "make his mark," it was an indication that he might be in trouble, and the officers on adjoining beats and the supervisor of the area would start a search for him. Walkie-talkie radios have largely replaced the need for this practice. Nevertheless, some departments—without being aware of the historical reason behind the practice—still require that both car and foot patrol officers call in hourly from particular locations on their beat. This practice also has roots in the watchman concept, especially in departments where the officers are required to make the phone calls from different call boxes. The primary purpose of this practice was to insure that the officer was moving about his assigned area rather than making all his calls from one location.

It seems reasonable to assume that persons planning some type of criminal activity would only need to observe the beat officer's method of patrolling for a short period before being able to predict where the officer will be at particular times if he patrols in a grid pattern or if he is required to make periodic phone checks.

If the department has identified the beat officer's role as being the eyes and ears of the department in addition to performing preventive patrol, it is essential that the officer combine the various methods of patrolling his beat so that they best serve his needs for whatever type of situation he is dealing with. The ability to suit the type of patrol he is conducting to the changing conditions and problems with which he will be dealing is the mark of an officer who has a thorough understanding of his beat and of his varying roles in relation to the beat.

In addition to knowing the geography of his beat fully, an officer's most effective tool is his knowledge of the identity of the persons who live, work, or hang out on his beat. The ability of an officer to communicate with persons on his beat and to gain their respect can be of invaluable assistance to him in keeping attuned to what is going on in the area. Business people are usually cooperative in passing information along to the officer relative to any persons or activities they feel are suspicious. Additionally, however, an officer can cultivate other sources of information. Experienced officers have long recognized the need to develop a relationship with the people who are most likely to have knowledge of criminal activities in the area. Gaining reliable sources of information from among such persons is usually a slow but rewarding undertaking. The success of an officer's attempts to develop such contacts will in the end depend on his understanding of people and his application of the concepts of psychology.

Recommended Reading

President's Commission on Law Enforcement and Administration of Justice, *Task Force Report: The Police* (Washington, D.C.: U.S. Government Printing Office, 1967), chapter 8. This chapter discusses recommendations for state commissions on minimum standards of training for police officers, and the types and extent of training that the commission believes are necessary.

CHAPTER 2

Preparation
for Duty

The fact that it is a daily practice makes it easy for an officer to neglect some area of preparation for going on duty. Such preparation properly starts before the officer leaves home, and includes such diverse areas as his personal dress, knowledge of his beat area, and a checkup of his police car.

Uniform and Equipment

In some localities it is still a common practice for officers either to wear their police uniform to and from work, or to wear some part of the uniform. Aside from the fact that using the official uniform as general wearing apparel indicates an unprofessional approach to his occupation, a patrol officer sometimes will receive a nonuniform assignment after he arrives at work, or even

17

during his work shift. The officer who is forced to wear some part of his police uniform will stand out conspicuously when he is attempting to be as inconspicuous as possible. An officer who wears his uniform tie or his uniform black shoes is easily spotted by the persons he would least want to identify him. Similarly, an officer who does not use an off-duty holster that will conceal his sidearm when he is dressed casually is at a definite disadvantage when he receives a nonuniform assignment.

An officer may be called to work on very short notice. He may not remember what parts of his uniform he brought home, or he may be away from home when he is notified to report for duty. Unless the officer has a complete uniform in his police locker he is likely to suffer embarrassment over his lack of full equipment.

Even a plainclothes officer, who is routinely assigned nonuniform duties, should have a complete uniform available at police headquarters. There may well be occasions when nonuniform officers will be given special assignments that will require their appearing in uniform.

Although a uniformed officer is easily identified by his dress and his police badge or shield, he should be prepared to have alternate methods of identification on him in the event that he is given a last-minute plainclothes assignment. Most departments, in addition to issuing a badge to each officer, also equip their officers with identification cards. This means of identification is of much more practical use when the officer may want only one or two persons in a crowded room to recognize his authority. Additionally, an officer normally assigned to uniform duty is likely to leave his badge on his uniform when he is in plain clothes. Without an alternate means of identification he may well find himself in a situation where he is suspected of being a criminal, or he may need to call for assistance from citizens and be unable to identify himself as a police officer.

Some officers, particularly those with small children, make it a habit to unload their service revolver whenever they take it home. Checking the weapon every time the officer prepares to go on duty should become as routine and important as putting on his clothes.

A reliable timepiece is equally important. The overall operation of a law enforcement agency is closely tied to the measurement of time. Aside from the basic situations in which an officer is expected to go on and off duty at particular times of the day or night, officers are routinely dispatched to meet individuals at specific locations at specific times. Whenever an officer is required to make a report, he must give the time of the incident. Or an officer may become aware of an incident that does not call for an official report but may be of importance at a later time; its importance may hinge on the time it occurred or on the time that an alleged witness claimed it occurred as opposed to the time the officer actually observed it.

Some officers assigned to uniform duty get in the habit of carrying little or no money when they report for duty. This practice is particularly prevalent in jurisdictions where officers are in the habit of accepting free meals and cigarettes while on duty. Other officers have such routine duties that they get in the habit of carrying their lunch or dinner to work with them. Again, if the officer should receive a last-minute assignment different from his routine duties, he should be prepared to carry out that assignment without having to make excuses to his commanding officer.

On a special assignment an officer might be required to work longer than his normal work shift. He might have to pose as a customer in a bar or restaurant where he would be expected to spend money. He may even have to hire a taxi or make a call to headquarters from a pay phone. In short, an officer should be financially prepared to carry out his role in whatever situation might develop. It is highly unlikely that a police department would not reimburse an officer who was forced to spend personal money to complete an investigation. Many such situations cannot be planned in advance so that the officer can be issued the money necessary before he goes out on the assignment.

Naturally, in addition to his uniform, the officer's locker at the police station should contain a replacement uniform and such necessary incidentals as extra shoelaces, extra ammunition, and extra flashlight batteries and bulbs. An officer who is prepared for the unexpected in his personal appearance is also training himself to be prepared for the unexpected in the line of duty.

The Assigned Area

While thorough familiarity with an area can only come through experience in working and patrolling it, an officer can avail himself of much useful information before he actually starts his patrol duties on a new beat. In all probability other officers who have worked the area will have personal bits of information that can be pieced together to give the newly assigned officer an indication of what to look for at different locations and at different times of the day or night. Such information includes the locations in which particular groups can be expected to congregate for conversation, dances, or meetings; if there are theaters on the beat, what time the shows let out; and potential problems or trouble spots. In the case of beats that contain industrial buildings, it is valuable for the officer to learn whether there are watchmen or private patrolmen on the premises and what hours they work.

In addition to information from fellow officers, the new beat patrolman can draw on several sources of recorded, formalized information that are available to the patrol officer in most departments. "Hot sheets," listing license numbers and/or descriptions of stolen cars, should be checked daily. Once an officer becomes familiar with these reports, he becomes adept at noticing which stolen cars are newly added to the list and which ones have been listed as stolen for a longer period of time. This type of knowledge, coupled with the officer's familiarity with his assigned beat, can be of great assistance to him when he spots cars parked in suspicious areas or parked at one location over an extended period of time. Additionally, general familiarity with the hot sheet can be of assistance when an officer receives a report of a crime recently committed and a description of the car involved.

A report of a recent robbery that includes a description of an auto previously reported as stolen is sometimes a tipoff to the officer that the car in question will be found abandoned in the general vicinity of the reported crime. Similarly, if an officer has already noticed a car parked in an unusual location prior to the robbery, it could possibly have been planted there so that the suspects could switch to it after abandoning the stolen car used in the robbery. In numerous cases officers have staked out a car under these circumstances and have been able to arrest suspects in the act of dumping their "hot" car and switching to the planted one.

On being newly assigned to a beat, an officer should always study the map of the area, not only to familiarize himself with the geographical make-up and boundaries of his beat, but also to ascertain the general boundaries of the adjoining beats. He should also know the locations of the main streets that pass from one beat to another. Additionally, knowledge of the most traveled streets and knowledge of back streets that can be used in getting to and from the same general locations served by the main streets are valuable tools to effective law enforcement.

Many patrol officers spend the great majority of their on-duty time patrolling the busiest streets in their assigned areas. This is due partly to subconscious habit and partly to the rationalization that areas having the most foot or vehicular traffic can reasonably be expected to present the most problems for a police officer. While this rationalization is undoubtedly true under some circumstances, it is equally true that a person who is fleeing from a crime recently committed, especially if he is somewhat experienced in avoiding the police, will avoid routes that would take him through streets that are likely to be patrolled.

On receiving a radio description of a car fleeing from the scene of a crime, some officers have had much success in moving away from the main streets and parking their patrol car with lights out in an area that commands a view of less frequented streets that pass through the beat. Parking the police car and devoting full attention to other autos as they approach and pass one location gives the officer a definite advantage over cruising an area in an attempt to spot a suspect auto while at the same time having to devote a part of his attention to normal traffic problems. This is especially true because of the many unpredictable reactions that both predestrians and drivers have when they are startled by the presence of a police car.

Other records that can afford the beat officer much useful information are the crime reports from his beat that have been filed within the last week or so. These reports can give the officer an insight into such problems as neighborhood feuds and the patterns (or lack of them) in burglaries and robberies. If an officer learns that a series of liquor store robberies has taken place in his assigned area over a relatively short period of time with somewhat the same modus operandi, or method of operation, it may indicate that he should pay particular attention to other such stores in his area that have not yet been victimized.

Such pre-patrol preparations quickly become routine to a good officer and indicate that he has a conscientious, professional approach to his job. As in any other endeavor, a person who has the drive to make good also prepares himself to the limit of his ability before he actually undertakes the task at hand.

The Police Car

One of the final pre-patrol preparations an officer should undertake is the inspection of his police car. In addition to ascertaining that the auto is in proper mechanical order and is sufficiently fueled, an officer should also be sure that the radio is in proper working order, that the spotlight and emergency lights work properly, and that the siren is in operating order.

In addition, however, one other type of inspection is vital, and if neglected can result in injury or death to an officer or the loss of a potential conviction in court. This is a thorough search by the officer of the inside of his patrol car, particularly the rear seat and any area that can be reached by a suspect who might be placed in the car during interrogation or while waiting to be transported to jail. Sometimes it is either impractical or illegal for the officer to conduct a thorough search of a person he places in his patrol car. In such instances the person being detained may secrete a weapon or some incriminating evidence in the car before it is found on him in a subsequent search. Or a person may conceal a weapon for use at a later time when the odds might be more in favor of an escape. There are even documented instances of suspects being placed in a police car, discovering a hidden weapon that was secreted by a previous occupant of the car, and then using this weapon to attempt to escape.

Aside from the possibility of physical injury to the police officer posed by a suspect's concealing a weapon in the police car, the officer should consider the possibility of suspects concealing potential incriminating evidence. In several cases officers have searched their cars after transporting or detaining suspects in it and found such evidence. In a recent California case the evidence consisted of marijuana cigarettes, which the officer had discovered after a suspect was removed from the car and then had placed in evidence. When the case came to trial it was established that the officer had not searched his car prior to placing the suspect in it and therefore could not testify that he had personal knowledge that the incriminating material was not in the car before the suspect was placed in it. This testimony resulted in dismissal of the charges and embarrassment to the officer that would not have come about if he had taken the precaution of checking his vehicle when he first went on duty.

Personal knowledge that some article of evidence was not in his car before a suspect was detained there has been exploited by experienced officers. In cases where the officer knows that he does not have legal authority to search a suspected person, he places the suspect in the rear of the patrol car and, after giving the suspect the impression that he is going to be searched, gives the suspect the opportunity to conceal some evidence or illegal material in the car. By this ruse the officer can deceive the suspect into producing evidence against himself that the officer would not otherwise be able to discover. After the suspect is given the opportunity to conceal the weapon or evidence, he is immediately removed from the car so that it may be searched and the incriminating material discovered in his presence. It is generally conceded that the act of immediately searching the car while the suspect is a witness to the search has a favorable effect on both prosecutor and jury.

In a particular case where this tactic was successful, the officers were assigned to respond to a report of a suspected check forger in a store. The owner of the business reported that the size of the check and the fact that the person writing the check had presented identification that appeared to be new had made him suspicious. While waiting for the arrival of the officers, the owner had assigned one of his employees to follow the suspect. When the suspect was located by the officers, he produced the check, but denied having any identification on him, claiming that he had inadvertently left it at home. The officers detained the suspect in the rear of their patrol car while they stood outside the car discussing the matter with the reporting citizen. Although the suspect had not been told that he was under arrest, his own guilty conscience apparently convinced him that he would be arrested and/or searched.

Meanwhile, the officers were aware that without reasonable cause on which to base an arrest, they had no legal justification for searching the suspect. Having thoroughly searched the passenger portion of their car before going on duty, they were deliberately offering the suspect an opportunity to get rid of any incriminating evidence he had on him. After several minutes of conversation between the officers and witnesses, the suspect was removed from the car, and it was searched in the presence of witnesses. In addition to several sets of identification cards bearing different names, they also found several blank checks that later proved to have been taken during a burglary. The officers were then in a position to make an arrest and to back that arrest up with both witnesses and evidence.

CHAPTER 3

Routine
Patrol
Practices

In his daily patrol duties, a police officer must do much more than simply cover his beat. He must make numerous observations, develop sources of information in the community, learn to know his community and be known in it, learn to recognize situations that are not what they appear, and recognize the effect his presence has on the people with whom he comes in contact.

Accurate Observations

The basis of good patrol is the ability of the officer to see and to interpret accurately the events going on around him. In order to assess accurately many incidents he observes, he must develop the ability to see without seeming to watch. It is understandable that many persons involved in some type of interaction with others tend to act or react differently if they know they are being observed by a police officer. Such a reaction can give an officer a false impression of what is actually taking place and will sometimes lull him into believing that nothing requiring his attention is taking place when in fact a crime may be either in progress or about to take place.

Examples of this type occur often in television dramas—a person is moving a dead or unconscious person down the street and acts as if he is helping a drunk friend for the benefit of a watching officer. Although this type of reaction to an observing officer is an exaggeration of the point, it should help show the officer that many things he observes during his routine patrol are acted out for his benefit.

Experienced officers develop the ability to appear to be disregarding some actions they have observed so that their presence will not hinder their ability to interpret the actions correctly. This may be done by watching the action in the reflection of a store window or in the rearview mirror of the police car as the officer drives away from the scene. Another ruse in getting suspects to believe that they are not under observation even though the officer is in the area is for the officer to busy himself with some other problem while at the same time keeping the suspects under observation without their knowledge. It is likely that they will then either attempt to remove themselves from his possible line of sight or make some other move that will confirm his suspicion that something is indeed going on.

Because an officer many times will get only a glimpse or a limited amount of time to observe a situation or to view particular persons, he needs to be able to make accurate observations and to recall these observations at a later time when it is convenient for him to record the facts in his notebook. The ability to describe a person physically and to describe his clothing in detail is an investigative tool that can assist in accurately analyzing the circumstances of a crime.

It is human nature for persons to be curious and to be attracted by the unusual, and it is normal that after observing such incidents the average person can give only a hazy description of what actually took place. An example of typical inattention to details was given a few years ago during a training lecture for police recruits. During a lecture by a police sergeant, a man burst into the classroom, cursed the sergeant, and attempted to attack him physically. Other officers rushed into the room to restrain the man, who was dragged away shouting at the sergeant, accusing him of running around with his wife. About ten minutes after the disturbance had been quelled and the lecture had been resumed, each of the recruits was asked to write a complete description of the sergeant's accuser. It was not until this moment that they realized that the act had been a training exercise, and none of them had noticed that the intruder was wearing only one shoe, had on no socks, was wearing a business suit with no shirt, and was wearing a tie around his bare neck.

Developing Sources of Information

Although paid informants are still a valuable source of information to the police officer, funds for such payments are usually restricted to officers assigned to investigative units, particularly for vice and narcotics investigations. Detectives usually develop such informants through their investigative contacts. In most instances the potential informant will offer his information to the officer in return for some assistance, ranging from interceding for the informant in an upcoming trial, in which the informant is charged with some criminal offense, to loaning the informant a few dollars. Once a man has offered to trade information for a loan or some other favor, he can usually be expected to be agreeable to selling valuable information for money.

Experience indicates that the average paid informant has a narrower scope of usable information than do many other people who may be willing to supply information. Many persons who can be encouraged to furnish information relative to criminal investigations become offended if the officer suggests that they be paid for their information. To these people the offering or accepting of money under such circumstances identifies them in their own eyes as a "fink" or a "snitch." Instead, they tend to have personal reasons for assisting the police. Such informants may be particularly repulsed by a certain type of crime or by the type of person who is the perpetrator of such crimes. Other informants are motivated by personal revenge or by the desire to get in the good graces of the police department or of a particular officer.

A new officer, or an officer newly assigned to a particular area, in addition to carrying himself in such a way as to encourage the respect of the citizens he comes in contact with, should not hold himself so aloof as to discourage potential sources of information from approaching him. Most guidelines for police officers stress that the officer should act in a manner intended to "enforce the law courteously without fear or favor ... and to respect the Constitutional rights of all men to liberty, equality, and justice."[1] This admonition should not be taken lightly. Contrary to this guideline, some officers operate as if under the impression that their uniform and gun demand respect from citizens. Such a misguided conception indicates an officer's basic misunderstanding, not only of his role as a police officer, but of the differences between respecting an individual for his personal qualities and accepting his lawful authority.

An officer who takes the time to know and converse with people of all classes and kinds on his beat not only is learning the character of his beat, but is affording potential sources of information the opportunity to contact him, to assess his sincerity and honesty, and to pass on information to him that not only can be of assistance to him in the performance of his duties but can conceivably be of benefit to him in protecting himself personally.

I have had a personal experience with this type of situation. While walking my beat, I was about to enter a place of business that was identified as a social club but was in actuality a gambling establishment. One of the co-owners of the operation contacted me on the street and suggested that I not enter the place alone. He went on to explain that a fugitive robbery suspect was inside and was known to be carrying a revolver in his pocket. (As mentioned earlier, potential informants tend to have other reasons than financial reward for passing information on to a police officer. The co-owner who told me the armed man was inside was well aware that it would be to the detriment of his business if violence occurred, particularly if it involved a police officer.)

In this particular city, illegal gambling was controlled more than suppressed, and when a hidden buzzer warned those inside that a police officer was entering, all money was cleared from the tables so that the occupants would appear to be playing a legal card game when the officer entered. Because I was prewarned, I was able to enter the place, and while ostensibly making a routine check of the premises, I was able to maneuver myself until the suspect—who was not aware that I knew his identity—was at a disadvantage and could not draw his gun when I informed him that he was under arrest.

Another type of informant the beat officer should cultivate is the person who is known to make his living from illegal activity but who is not actually wanted. Some officers feel that it is their duty to harass such a person in order to make it clear that although the officer does not have reasonable cause to arrest him, he knows him to be involved in criminality. Experience has shown, however, that many people who fall into the category of "professional" criminals tend also to have a "professional" approach to a police officer's duty and, if treated with common courtesy rather than contempt or unnecessary force by an officer, will acknowledge their respect of the officer by making valuable information available to him.

An important aspect of developing sources of information involves the officer's recognition of the need to use different approaches in dealing with different potential informants. Some informants may be willing to approach an officer openly with no concern for their being seen talking to him. Others, while willing to cooperate with the officer, feel that if they are seen associating with him they will be labeled as a "snitch." The officer thus must be both flexible and alert so that he can give a potential informant the opportunity to set up a contact with him and to pass on information.

In some instances an informant will acknowledge the officer's presence but will not approach him, and may walk off shortly after the officer's arrival. This may be a signal that the man wishes to talk to the officer privately. Or a potential informant may engage the officer in a seemingly innocent or meaningless conversation while sparring for time. In this type of situation the officer must "play it by ear" and give the informant the opportunity to signal his intentions.

Regardless of the type of approach the informant takes, the officer should be alert for cues. If, for some reason, he feels it is inadvisable for him to talk to the informant at that time, he should make the informant aware of this. The mere act of warning the informant off sometimes serves to gain future cooperation from him because of his belief that the officer is concerned with protecting the confidentiality of their relationship.

Knowing and Being Known in the Community

Persons who live and/or work in a community generally like to know the police officer assigned to their area. They want to feel that they can approach the officer, both informally as acquaintances do when they meet and exchange light conversation, and also when they have a problem and seek the officer's advice or professional involvement. People appreciate being recognized by name and the more people in his area that the beat officer can call by name, the more persons he will have who are potential sources of cooperation or information. Many persons are flattered by the mere fact that the officer approaches them and calls them by name when he requests information or assistance. To such persons, the pride they feel in being recognized by an officer in the presence of their friends or acquaintances will encourage them to go out of their way in attempting to be of assistance to the officer to justify his approaching them.

Just as some persons feel complimented by such inquiries from an officer, other persons who would otherwise be cooperative tend to resent being put on the spot for information by the officer in the presence of other persons. If the beat officer takes the time to know the people in his area, he can not only develop sources of information, but can classify these sources so that he will know who will be likely to have certain types of information and in what way these people should be approached.

Recognizing Deliberate Distractions

As mentioned earlier, an officer must be able to observe suspicious activities without allowing his presence to generate false clues from the persons involved. In addition, the officer must be alert for false clues or attempts by persons to distract his attention from some suspicious activity. For example, an officer may stop a car in connection with some type of investigation or simply for a traffic violation. Usually under such circumstances the driver of the car will pull to the curb or the side of the road and wait for the officer to approach on foot. At other times, however, the driver will quickly get out and walk back to the police car. He might vehemently argue his innocence of any traffic violation or simply engage the officer in conversation while voluntarily producing his identification. When the driver goes back to the police car quickly, he may only be trying to impress the officer with his willingness to cooperate, hoping to elicit sympathy from the officer and get only a verbal warning rather than a traffic citation. He may also want to plead for leniency, or sympathy, away from the passengers in his car so that he will not lose face.

Aside from these relatively innocent reasons, however, the driver who leaves his car may be attempting to distract the officer or to conceal something by making it unnecessary for the officer to come close to the stopped auto. Under such circumstances it is usually prudent for the officer to take his time and not to indicate that he sees anything unusual in the driver's actions. If a cover car is available, the officer should request cover and make a closer examination only after such cover has arrived. If he has to deal with the situation alone, he should attempt to evaluate the situation thoroughly before he makes his move. If he feels that further examination of the car and/or its passengers is called for, he should first notify the police dispatcher of his exact location and the fact that he is checking out a suspicious auto and occupants. Still without seeming to have any abnormal suspicions, the officer should approach the car in such a way as to afford himself as much protection as possible, while at the same time keeping its occupants—and the driver—under observation.

Sometimes the officer may justifiably feel that discretion is the better part of valor—if the stop were made at night in a sparsely populated area, for example, or if it were in a commercial area with little or no probability that any other witnesses would be present. At such times he should not approach the car but should obtain all the information possible from the driver. Even if the suspect auto is allowed to drive off without the officer's making a close examination of it or its passengers, he has gained potentially important information. Identity of the driver, the number and general description of the passengers, and the description of the car may well be valuable in a subsequent investigation.

Other types of distractions that have been used to divert police officers include amorous couples in parked cars who make no attempt to acknowledge the officer's approach, and persons who engage in a scuffle in view of an approaching officer or police car. A pair of apparent lovers can in actuality be lookouts for some criminal activity, or one person can be attempting to conceal the actual condition of the other from the police officer. In approaching them, the officer should first make sure that he has the parties in his full view and then deliberately attract their attention by knocking on the window of the car or, if it is at night, shining his flashlight at them.

In the case of a scuffle that the officer has reason to suspect is an act for his benefit, he should slow his approach and thoroughly check the surrounding area for evidence of some activity from which the scuffling persons might be attempting to distract him. Even if he notices no other suspicious activity, he should approach the fighters carefully and make them aware of his presence without coming in contact with them or within their reach.

An officer should never rush blindly into any situation. Sounds of gunshots, screams, or running should be interpreted as an indication that something unusual is taking place, but should not evoke an unplanned or careless reaction from the officer. In a recent case a police officer heard the sounds of gunshots from a small grocery store and saw two men, the second one armed, run from the store. The officer opened fire on the man with the gun, seriously wounding him, only to discover that the man was the owner of the store who was chasing a man who had just robbed him.

In another case, an officer responded to a report of a rape in progress in an apartment house. Hearing screams and sounds of a struggle on his arrival outside the door of the apartment, he forced the locked door open by firing his shotgun at the doorknob. In the process he killed the woman who was the victim of the attack.

Reactions to an Officer's Presence

One of the skills a new officer can begin to develop his first day on a beat is the ability to "read" the people he observes or meets.

It is probable, particularly if the beat includes a large number of business places, that the people on the beat will come from numerous ethnic and socioeconomic backgrounds. Given these varying backgrounds, the population will in all probability display attitudes toward the officer that will range from deep resentment to total fear and/or respect.

While emphasizing that his role is to assist citizens as well as to deter or prevent crime, the individual officer should develop his own relationship with the people on the beat in such a way that they will recognize him as an individual with whom they can communicate and upon whom they can call for assistance. The officer should make it his business to learn the backgrounds of those who display a particular like, dislike, or fear of his position. To break down stereotyped prejudices that any of these persons have against the police, it is first necessary to understand—even though he may not agree with—the basis for their attitudes or feelings.

A potentially touchy problem with which the beat officer may be faced is the individual who is overly willing to cooperate and furnish information. Many times such persons feel a reflected glory or importance in having a close association with a police officer. They may manufacture reasons and excuses for talking to the officer. An officer new to a beat should be cautious in handling such individuals. Some persons who seemingly go out of their way to be friendly or helpful to an officer have a self-serving motive. The friendly "informant" may be attempting to impress others with his rapport with the officer or his ability to obtain information from the officer. In some such instances, such individuals are "contact men" who have been given the responsibility for offering the officer a deal or a payoff in return for his cooperation. If such a contact man can assure that he is observed in conversation with the officer, it is no great problem for him to manufacture information that he can claim was passed on to him. By giving the officer false information to attract his attention elsewhere, the contact can claim that he actually paid the officer to stay away from a particular location while some illegal act took place there.

One of the best ways for an officer to protect himself from being placed in such a situation is to learn all he can about persons offering him unsolicited assistance or information. He should attempt to discover what benefit the informant could logically expect for his information. What is the person's background? Does he have a criminal record? If so, what type of criminal activity does it involve? Who are his associates? Is his information useful or reliable? In short, by being suspicious and questioning the informant's motives, the officer can often both protect himself and determine the informant's reliability.

Occasionally the officer will have official dealings that relate to the personal problems of individuals on his beat or that involve intimate problems in their family life. It is particularly important in such cases that the officer develop a reputation for being both closemouthed and understanding. An officer with sensitive information about a person's personal life should not let his information affect his relationship with that person. When an individual about whom an officer has sensitive or potentially embarrassing information realizes that possession of the information has not changed the officer's attitude or relationship toward him, he is likely to view the officer as a highly competent professional, to be respected, trusted, and confided in.

A reputation for being closemouthed, professional, and yet understanding is particularly important to an officer when his official responsibilities overlap his social life. As important as it is for an officer to refrain from divulging official information to persons he sees socially, it is perhaps more important for him to refrain from using information gained in his private or social life in his professional capacity.

In the long run, if an officer learns that he might be put in the position in a police investigation of using information gained in contacts with personal friends or associates, it is better for him to request of his superiors that he not be involved in any such investigation. Although many authorities stress that a police officer is theoretically on duty twenty-four hours a day, it is generally recognized that an officer also has an overriding need to keep his social and private lives separate from his professional role. The surest way for an officer to alienate himself and his family from the community is to get the reputation for being willing to spy on his friends and neighbors in order to benefit himself professionally.

This is one of the primary reasons why, in larger departments, officers are seldom assigned to duty in areas in which they live. Police administrators believe that such assignments work too much of a hardship on the officer and that the stresses and pressures of the police role are such that officers should have the maximum opportunity to have a social life completely apart from their role as a police officer.

How to Patrol a Beat

As mentioned earlier, two primary purposes of beat patrol are to make the residents and employees of an area aware of the police presence and to increase the officer's probability of being in the vicinity of a crime in progress or of actually being in a position to apprehend persons who commit or attempt criminal acts.

Some officers feel that the best approach to patrolling a beat is to circulate throughout the beat as rapidly and as often as possible. This approach requires constant driving on the officer's part, with little time spent in citizen contacts or in sitting back and observing activities. The most practical approach is to strike a compromise between constant overall coverage of the beat and spending time in citizen contact and observations from a fixed location. In addition to the officer's—or the police vehicle's—presence alerting potential criminals, patrol from a moving vehicle markedly inhibits the officer's ability to observe activities in detail.

The average beat contains a combination of business and residential buildings. Particularly from a public relations point of view, the police officer should be seen periodically in the residential areas of his beat. Obviously, he is most easily seen during daylight hours, but the swing shift officer should also make it a point to circulate through such areas during the early evening hours when there is still likely to be some outdoor activity by the residents.

Late at night and during periods of inclement weather, there is likely to be relatively little activity in residential areas, and therefore the officer can devote more time to the more active areas of his beat. This does not mean, however, that the officer should totally abandon patrolling residential areas late at night. Different situations dictate different patrol patterns, and the officer should vary his pattern of covering his assigned area.

As he becomes more familiar with his assigned beat, the officer will naturally become familiar with the areas that are likely to call for the most attention. He will also learn which locations—particularly business or commercial structures—are most attractive or vulnerable to thefts or burglaries. The officer should make periodic checks of such locations, paying particular attention to any unusual activity or traffic in the area. In some instances an unattended parked auto in a commercial area late at night is an indication of illegal activity. Particularly if no one is around the car and the hood is warm to the touch, the officer should be suspicious. His first action should be to check out the car to ascertain whether it has been reported stolen. A stolen car may either be abandoned in a quiet area or be used as part of a crime. Even if the officer learns that the car has not been reported stolen, he is justified in remaining suspicious. The auto could have been stolen but its loss not yet discovered by the owner, or the license plates could have been switched in order to delay any police check on its ownership.

The practices of altering his route and time schedule, and of periodically "laying in" at a fixed location cannot be overstressed. The officer conducting a moving patrol should base 50 percent of his effectiveness on being seen and the other 50 percent on what he can see. By contrast, an officer who parks his car to minimize its visibility while he observes the activity in the area has a 100 percent effectiveness in his ability to direct all his attention to the activities around him. An officer who, through his experience, can make an intelligent judgment as to the probability of a criminal act being committed at a particular location, and then spend his time watching that location, is far more likely to discover a crime in progress than the officer who is continually on the move in the hope that he will luckily be at the right location at the right time.

CHAPTER 4

Proper
Radio
Procedure

The elements of good radio procedure are brevity, clarity, and explicitness. In situations of stress or excitement, some officers are prone to forget one or all of these important factors. Misuse of the police radio can result—and has resulted—in confusion, failure to apprehend a suspect who would otherwise have been captured, and death or injury to police officers. It is obvious, therefore, that proper radio procedure is not merely a bureaucratic tool to induce uniformity but it is an essential part of police operations, both for increased professionalism within the department and for protection of individual officers.

Police departments have become increasingly aware that proper radio procedure begins with the police dispatcher at the base transmitting station. Additionally, it is apparent that dispatchers who have first-hand awareness of the problems faced by the officer on the street exhibit a feeling for their responsibilities that makes possible increased coordination and effectiveness between the dispatcher and the officer on the street.

Most departments use a three-way transmission method by which the base station can talk to the field units and the field units can transmit to the base station and can also contact other field units. Larger departments transmit on two, three, or more channels in order to minimize the possibility of overloading transmissions on one channel.

The problem common to most types of police radio communications is that when any one unit is transmitting, he either wholly or partially blocks out any other transmissions. In addition, when a field unit is transmitting, he blocks out all reception by his own receiver as long as his transmitter is on. This seems like a minor point, but surprisingly many new officers are unaware of it. Some new officers assume—and some older officers act as if—their police radio is a telephone and that it is proper to use it for two-way narrative-type conversations. Unfortunately, the importance of proper radio procedures may only be recognized after improper radio use has caused a breakdown in police operations. In numerous instances an officer has been unable to call for assistance in apprehending a fleeing suspect because another unit was monopolizing the radio with an unnecessarily long and relatively unimportant transmission. Of more importance is the fact that officers have been killed or injured because of their inability to call for assistance while being blocked out by transmission of other units.

Obviously, there have been and will continue to be instances in which transmissions will be prevented simply because of equally or more important transmissions by other units. The point, however, is that by using proper radio procedures, and by using the police radio only when necessary, departments have been able to cut down on their total transmission time by as much as 50 percent. This means that the officer on the street has a much greater chance to get his transmissions through.

Some of the more common examples of misuse of the police radio involve the beat officer transmitting messages for the convenience of citizens: "Citizen would like to know if we have a missing persons report for a Mary Doe" or "Citizen would like to know if we have a William Smith in custody." Obviously there are more practical methods by which such information can be obtained, and in any event the police radio should not be used for such routine information. When a citizen is attempting to obtain nonemergency information, the beat officer generally should advise him either to inquire in person at police headquarters or to phone in for the information. Sometimes a citizen asks an officer to make inquiries of this kind for him because the person himself does not want to become involved. As standard procedure, some departments require any citizen attempting to obtain such information to identify himself and will not give information relating to arrests or missing persons over the phone.

Officers themselves initiate many unnecessary transmissions. Sometimes the request for another unit's location is simply for the purpose of getting together for a cup of coffee. Similarly, if an officer is attempting to ascertain whether an apparently abandoned auto has been reported stolen, rather than using the police radio—a process that will usually involve at least four separate transmissions between the field unit and the base station—it would be much simpler for the officer to request the needed information by telephone, usually the police call box.

Obviously, different departments have different guidelines for acceptable radio transmission. Underlying all the rules, however, is the general principle that the police radio should be reserved for transmissions of an emergency nature in which the situation dictates the use of radio rather than land-wire transmissions.

Radio transmissions are primarily intended for the assignment of units for investigative purposes or for other patrol-related duties. Additionally, the police radio is used as a means of ascertaining the location of various units. Whenever an officer is going to leave his car he usually notifies his station of his location and the purpose for leaving his car. Such a call not only notifies the station that he is unavailable for assignment, but also lets other cars in the area know his location in the event that he needs assistance. Some departments require that on any official action the officer is about to undertake, he is to notify the station of his location and the type of situation. This would include such activities as car stops for traffic citations, stopping to eat, and stopping at a police call box to telephone in to headquarters.

The historical background of police radio communications is

relatively brief. The first radios installed in police vehicles were receivers only. The first operational police radio system was operated by the Detroit Police Department in 1928. It consisted of a transmitter installed on Belle Isle in the Detroit River and a receiver set installed in the rear seat of one cruiser car. The radio operator would transmit his messages "in the blind" and hope that the cruiser car received them.

These first hesitant steps into a new era of police work were hampered by lack of sensitivity of the receiving set and considerable red tape as to rules and guidelines, which at that time were enforced by the Federal Radio Commission. In spite of this, within three years twenty-three police departments had their own transmitting stations. It wasn't until 1933, however, that the first two-way, mobile police radio system was operational. It was operated by the Bayonne, New Jersey, department.

In 1945, after the development of mobile, two-way FM transmitters and receivers, the Federal Communications Commission assigned frequencies for FM, and FM was adopted as the overall system for police radio communications. The overall success of the two-way and three-way police radios has led first to equipping police motorcycles with similar equipment, and more recently to the development of walkie-talkie radios for foot patrolmen. Still more recently some departments have begun equipping their prowl car officers with walkie-talkie radios to give them increased range and flexibility of operations. Under this setup, officers assigned to car patrol need no longer worry about first notifying the base station—and possibly losing valuable time while waiting for an opportunity to transmit—before leaving their car to make an investigation on foot. With the walkie-talkie they are still able to summon assistance or cover and to receive transmissions from headquarters.

As effective as these methods of communication have proven to be as a law enforcement aid or tool, they have also served to further whet the appetites of police administrators. More and more highly sophisticated and highly technical communications equipment is being devised for increasing the efficiency of law enforcement agencies and aiding the individual officer in the performance of his duties. Many departments have a computer hooked into other major departments in the state, so they can almost instantly get back information relative to previous crime reports, missing persons, suspects, and stolen cars. Some departments even have similar computers installed in the patrol cars, allowing the individual officers to make such checks without the delay of going through the police radio system.

Before concluding a discussion of proper radio procedure, attention should be given to a basic and fundamental problem in oral communications—namely, the possibility of being misunderstood. A good radio communicator uses careful pronunciation and uses the phonetic alphabet when a word or spelling is likely to be difficult to understand or to be misunderstood. Anytime the radio dispatcher fails to understand a transmission from a field unit he is forced to request the unit to repeat his transmission. This at least doubles the amount of time required for the transmission and, more important, decreases proportionally the time available for transmissions by other units.

One of the most important prerequisites of proper radio communications is for the officer to know what he wants to say in its entirety before he activates his transmitter. There is nothing more disconcerting to other units than to have a unit's transmitter come on the air and, after a few moments of silence, to hear the officer groping and trying to decide just how to phrase his message or request. By spending a few minutes organizing his thoughts before he activates his transmitter, an officer will have much smoother transmissions and will receive more assistance from the base station. A transmission in which the officer identifies himself and briefly states his problem or the information he desires is much more easily understood and acted upon than is a long, rambling dissertation from which the dispatcher must extract the pertinent information or facts.

Compare these two transmissions: (1) "Dispatcher, this is unit 12. I have a car stopped, and I'd like you to run a check to ascertain if it is stolen or if we have any reports on it. It's a blue over green Buick, 1967 or 1968; it's a four-door; and the license number is MVC 123." (2) "Unit 12 calling. License and Identification check on Mable, Victor, Charlie 123." The second transmission contains all the information necessary for the radio room to use in checking out the auto. If there is any question whether the license plates belong to that particular car the matter is resolved when the dispatcher gives back the requested information. He will repeat the license number, describe the auto to which it is registered (1967 blue over green Buick Skylark four-door, registered to James Smith, 400 Overlook Drive, this city). If any of the information coming back is contrary to the facts known to the requesting officer, he knows that he has the basis for a further inquiry.

CHAPTER 5

Reports and the Police Notebook

Good reports are an asset both to the individual officer and to other officers involved in an investigation. In addition to a police report being a permanent record of an incident or crime, it is the report to which other investigators—police, insurance, attorneys —turn to obtain the facts.

The accuracy of reports submitted by the police officer is of great importance, not only as they relate to a particular crime or investigation, but as reference points for future judgments on any studies relating to operational practices and guidelines. Additionally, one of the primary methods of judging an officer's efficiency is to evaluate his reports.

Most police departments have structured forms for reporting various incidents. (See Figure 1.) This assures uniformity in both the type of information that will be furnished and the sequence in which the information will be recorded. While having a common sequence of information on all reports may seem a small matter, it is not. A great deal of investigation is done by reading numerous reports to attempt to find common factors that may be a key to an overall modus operandi. An investigator may be interested only in knowing at what hour a series of crimes occurred, or what weapons were used in a series of robberies. Reading completely through a stack of reports to locate such information is both time-consuming and time-wasting.

Accuracy

To be of any benefit, police reports must be accurate. This requires that the reporting officer clearly distinguish between supposition and fact. While it is not always possible for the officer to be absolutely accurate as to the date, time, or location of an incident, he can indicate in his report a span of dates or times and indicate that a location is approximate or assumed. Also, the officer should indicate clearly whether the information is recorded as fact or as information received from some other source. In such cases, the source furnishing the information should be identified.

An example of the use of a span of dates or times would be a report of the discovery of a dead body. Except in unusual cases the officer is not going to be able to ascertain the exact date and time of death for his report. By on-the-scene investigation and interrogations, however, he can in all probability fix the time of death between two specific points. In many cases some interested party notifies the police that the subject has not been seen recently. This person is usually able to furnish the officer with the date and approximate time the deceased was last seen alive. The date-time span would begin at that point and continue to the date and time of the discovery of the body.

In a robbery or homicide it may be important to indicate the time of the offense as closely as possible. In such instances, while the reporting officer may still find it necessary to indicate a span of time, he can narrow the span considerably by finding out the exact time that the offense was first reported to the police prior to his being dispatched to the scene.

INCIDENT REPORT				1. COMPLAINANT'S NAME (LAST, FIRST, MIDDLE)		2. COMPLAINT NO.
METROPOLITAN POLICE DEPT., WASH., D. C.				HOLT LEE May		▸
14. EX. COPIES	15. DIST.	16. BEAT	17. R.A.	3. STREET ADDRESS	N/W	4. HOME PHONE
/	▸ 4	6	12	25 Skyview		© 625 1077
18. COMP. OCCUPATION - HRS. EMPLOYED				5. WHERE EMPLOYED - SCHOOL ATTENDING		6. BUS. PHONE
▸ Printer 0900 - 1745				2710 Georgia Ave NW		636 6624
19. TYPE OF PREMISE				7. SEX	DOB	8. CRIME OR INCIDENT
Street				▸ M	16 Feb 31	▸ ADW
20. VEHICLE HELD - TAG NO. STATE & YR.				9. LOCATION OF CRIME/INCIDENT (ADDRESS)	N S E W	10. DATE, DAY & TIME
none				▸ IFO 1500 16ᵗʰ St NW		10 Jun 2100 S-M-T-W-T-F-S
21. MAKE YEAR MODEL COLOR				11. WEAPON, TOOL, FORCE OR MEANS USED (DESCRIBE)		PHOTOS
				Knife		▸ NO ☐ YES FS#
CODE C O-OWNER C-COMPLAINANT P-PARENT/GUARDIAN R-REPORTING PERSON				12. METHOD USED		13. CLASSIFICATION (OFF)
				Striking		▸
22. NAME (LAST, FIRST, MIDDLE)			CODE	RES. ADDRESS	HOME PHONE	BUS. PHONE
23.						
24.						

25. IF ANIMAL BITE, GIVE INOCULATION NO.   LIC. NO.   IF IMPOUNDED DATE AND TIME

26. IDENTIFY SUSPECTS BY NUMBER, NAME, ADDRESS, SEX, RACE, AGE, HEIGHT, WEIGHT, EYES, HAIR, ETC. IF ARRESTED GIVE ARREST NUMBER AND CHARGE. IF ANIMAL GIVE KIND, SIZE, COLOR, ETC.

NAME	ADDRESS
(1)	

SEX	RACE	AGE	HT	WT	EYES	HAIR	CLOTHING
M	W	20-25	5'10	140	BRN	BLK	Dark pants + jacket

(2)

27. NATURE OF INJURY AND LOCATION ON BODY   ▸ Knife wound in Left arm (laceration)   28. IF HOSPITALIZED - WHERE? ☐ ADMITTED ☐ RELEASED

29. TRANSPORTED BY: ▸   30. TREATED BY: self

NARRATIVE: COMPLETE ALL APPROPRIATE ITEMS. USE SPACE BELOW TO (1) CONTINUE ABOVE ITEMS AS NECESSARY INDICATING ITEM NUMBER AT LEFT. (2) BRIEFLY DESCRIBE INCIDENT AND ACTION TAKEN. (3) DESCRIBE EVIDENCE OR PROPERTY AND INDICATE DISPOSITION. (4) IF MORE SPACE IS NEEDED USE CONTINUATION REPORT.

ITEM NO.

Compl. stated he was walking home from theatre when susp #1 approached + asked for a cigarette. Comp. attempted to walk away + susp. cut him on left arm. Susp. then fled on foot south on 16ᵗʰ St. Comp has feminine mannerisms + is vague on details surrounding the incident. Although wound was bleeding there was no blood on C's clothes

T.T. NUMBER	DATE & TIME THIS REPORT	32. DATE/TIME TYPE NO.	33. REPRODUCE NO.
	10 Jun 2200		
34. REPORTING OFFICER, UNIT & BADGE NO.	35. STATUS (CHECK ONE)	36. UNIT REFERRED TO	37. UCR DISPOSITION
G Pearson 5410C	☐ OPEN ☐ CLOSED ☐ UNFOUNDED ☐ SUSPENDED		
38. SECOND OFFICER - UNIT & BADGE NO.	39. SUPERVISOR APPROVING UNIT & BADGE NO.	40. REVIEWER	NO.

PD 253 - REVISED 10/73   J-5382-74

Figure 1

Opinions *Versus* Facts

While some persons in the law enforcement field hold that individual opinions do not belong in an official police report, others recognize that police officers are assumed to be skilled and knowledgeable in their occupation. To insist that they submit reports that do not reflect their professional opinions not only limits the follow-up investigator's knowledge of the situation but deprives him of the insights of a trained observer who was at the scene. It is imperative, however, that opinions, conclusions, or educated guesses be identified as such in the report.

For example, suppose a citizen reported to an officer that he had been beaten and robbed but exhibited no bruises or torn or dirty clothes. If the officer was of the opinion that the reporting person was fabricating all or part of his story for some ulterior purpose, the inclusion of the opinion in the narrative portion of his report could be of great assistance to the follow-up investigator. On the other hand, if the reporting officer did not mention his opinion, the follow-up investigator would be unaware of a possible vital point when he interviewed the victim at a later date. At the very least the investigator would have been deprived of the investigative tool of offering the alleged victim the opportunity to further fabricate his story by asking him what injuries or damages to his clothing he suffered.

In short, an investigative lead in the case would have been lost through a requirement that the reporting officer only deal with facts. Above all, the reporting officer should have both the leeway and the ability to describe accurately in the report a situation or condition he observed. The purpose of the report is not to convict or exonerate but to provide facts and observations that might be pertinent at a later date.

At the same time, an officer should be aware that he can be challenged for overstating his factual knowledge of a situation in court, particularly if his statement is not clearly identified as opinion rather than fact. In a homicide case, for example, the reporting officer might state in his report that he found the victim dead, or that the victim died in his presence. In a trial, a defense attorney—and in some instances a prosecuting attorney—would be quick to question the accuracy of such a statement on the grounds that the officer is not a medical expert and therefore is not qualified to pronounce death. Experienced officers, rather than fall into this trap, will state that the victim *appeared* dead. It is usually assumed that the officer can recognize apparent death.

Other examples of areas in which the officer should take care not to overstate his facts are in the reporting of the time of an offense and in describing sounds. In investigation of an explosion or burglary, an officer might find evidence—such as a disconnected electric clock—that might have been disconnected at the time of the offense. The officer could reasonably assume that the time indicated on the clock was the time that the offense occurred. He should keep in mind, however, that this is only an assumption and that he should in no instance state it in his report as a fact. In his report, the officer could state: "The electric clock, which may have been damaged or disconnected at the time of the offense, was stopped at 1415 hours." The officer should keep in mind the possibility that the perpetrator could have reset the time on the clock in order to cover his tracks or in order to provide someone with an alibi.

Several times officers have been tripped up in court when questioned about their reports of the sounds of gunshots. An officer who states that he heard gunshots in a specific situation is very likely to be asked how he knew the sounds were gunshots rather than firecrackers or the sounds of an auto backfiring. This problem could easily be avoided if the officer merely stated that he heard what *sounded like* gunshots.

Written Record of the Crime Scene

In addition to completing the official written report, an officer should also record pertinent facts of a case in his own notebook. It is important that this record be in the officer's own handwriting and that the notes be written either at the time of observations were made or very shortly thereafter. (See Figure 2.)

It is highly unlikely that an officer can foresee at the time of an incident all the information and details that he may be called upon to recall later. For this reason many experienced officers include as a format in their notes the answers to the questions

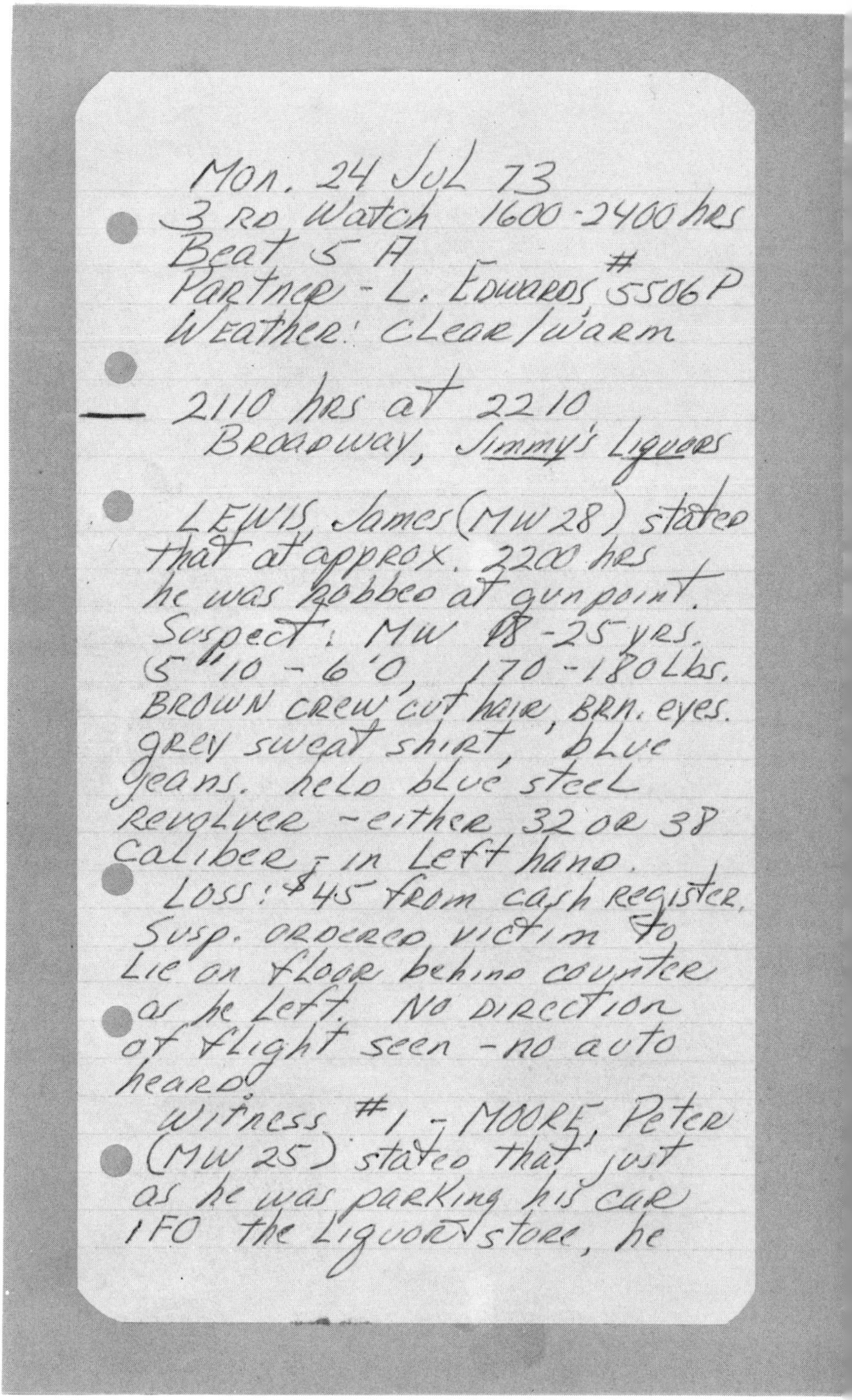

Mon. 24 Jul 73
3 rd Watch 1600-2400 hrs
Beat 5 A
Partner - L. Edwards #5506 P
Weather: clear/warm

2110 hrs at 2210
Broadway, Jimmy's Liquors

Lewis, James (MW 28) stated
that at approx. 2200 hrs
he was robbed at gunpoint.
Suspect: MW 18-25 yrs.
5"10 - 6'0, 170-180 Lbs.
Brown crew cut hair, Brn. eyes.
grey sweat shirt, blue
jeans. held blue steel
revolver - either 32 or 38
caliber - in left hand.
Loss: $45 from cash register.
Susp. ordered victim to
lie on floor behind counter
as he left. No direction
of flight seen - no auto
heard.
Witness #1 - Moore, Peter
(MW 25) stated that just
as he was parking his car
IFO the liquor store, he

Figure 2

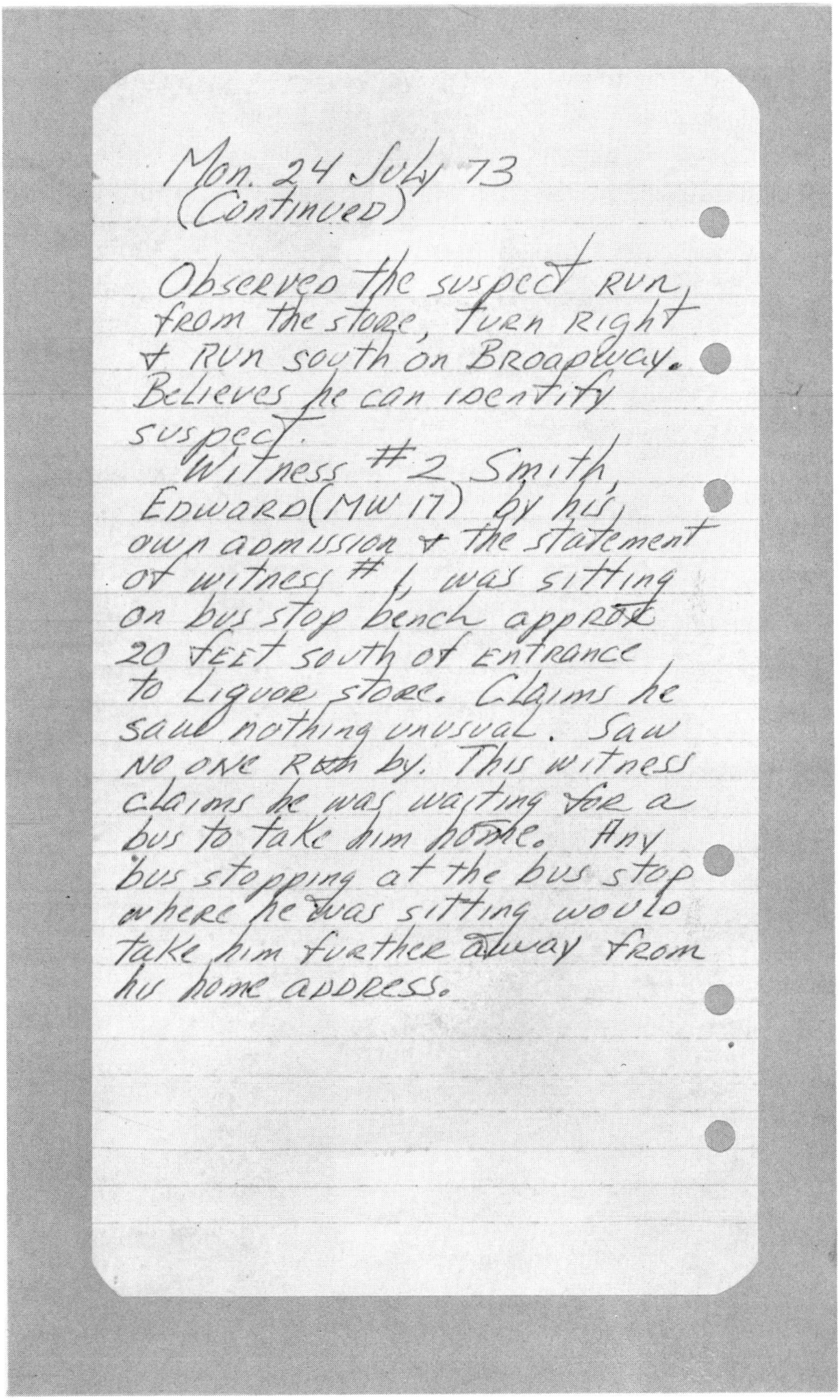

Mon. 24 July 73
(Continued)

Observed the suspect run
from the store, turn right
+ run south on Broadway.
Believes he can identify
suspect.
Witness #2, Smith,
Edward (MW 17) by his
own admission + the statement
of witness #1, was sitting
on bus stop bench approx
20 feet south of entrance
to liquor store. Claims he
saw nothing unusual. Saw
no one run by. This witness
claims he was waiting for a
bus to take him home. Any
bus stopping at the bus stop
where he was sitting would
take him further away from
his home address.

Figure 2 (continued)

who, what, why, when, where, and how. Additionally, depending on the circumstances and the type of case, it may be helpful to record such information as the weather at the time of the incident, the lighting conditions, and the names of witnesses. It is also often useful to note or summarize what each witness reported that he did or did not observe or hear. What a witness claimed he did not see or hear can be at least as important as what he said he did see or hear, because witnesses sometimes change their stories from their stated original observations.

Admissibility of Notes in Court

Most criminal courts allow an officer to refer to his notes in order to refresh his memory while he is on the witness stand, provided the notes were personally written by the officer at the time of or shortly after the incident. Some officers have been prevented from making such use of their notes because the notes were typewritten. The court held that typewritten notes were in all probability made a considerable time after the incident and therefore were susceptible to hindsight and evaluations that rendered them less reflective of the officer's actual observations at the time he made them.

A point of confusion in crime scene notetaking is at least partly attributable to a well-known text on criminal investigation.[1] This text recommends that two officers work as a team at a crime-scene investigation and that one officer make all the observations and dictate them to his partner, who records them in the notebook. This text goes on to explain that this method allows both officers to use the notes in court later. Unfortunately, this is not always true. In practice, when an officer attempts to use notes while testifying, one of the first questions he is likely to be asked is, "Did you personally make these notes?" Unless the answer is yes, the attorney can successfully prevent the use of the notes. Similarly, unless the officer can state that he not only made the notes but also personally made the observations, he can again be prevented from using them.

The officer should also be aware that once he is allowed to make use of his notes while on the witness stand, the defense attorney has the right to examine the notes and can use them in an attempt to impeach the officer's testimony. It is primarily for this reason that the notebook should be of the loose-leaf type to allow the officer to remove only those notes he will be using during his testimony. By doing this, he limits the defense attorney to examining just those notes and does not afford him the opportunity to examine the whole notebook.

One such case in which the officer's testimony was impeached occurred because the defense was able to examine the entire notebook and was able to show that the notes the officer claimed were recorded shortly after the offense were written in ink of a different color from that used for other entries on the same date and on dates both before and after the incident in question. Obviously the inference was that the officer had made up and inserted the notes in his book at a later date in order to substantiate his testimony. It is equally important that notes in the officer's book be made in ink. This tends to avoid the question of whether erasures were made at a later date.

When to Make Notes

Obviously, it is to the officer's advantage to make notes whenever he is required to take some official action. Modern police work is such that officers are constantly required to make nearly instant decisions and to defend their judgment for those decisions later. An officer who is methodical and accurate in his notetaking therefore has an additional tool to substantiate his judgment and the reasonableness of his decisions and actions.

Not only should the officer record his actions, but he should also make written entries covering any observations he feels may have later significance. At times an officer will observe an individual or an auto that provokes his suspicions but that he feels does not warrant any action on his part at the time. The mere act of recording the license number and description of the car or the physical description and dress of a person, along with a record of the date, time, and circumstances, has often developed into a most important piece of evidence in a subsequent investigation.

The beat or patrol officer himself has almost unlimited use for his own notes. Aside from keeping a written record of his activities, he can use his notes in future and unrelated investigations. For example, suppose an officer has reason to interrogate two males in an auto under what he feels are suspicious circumstances. In his notebook he records the subjects' identities and the description of the car. Nothing comes of this incident, but months later he arrests one of the subjects in the same car, attempting to flee from the scene of a burglary. A witness states that he observed two men at the burglary scene. The officer's previous suspicions, which caused him to record the identities of both subjects, may well lead to identifying and capturing the second suspect.

Officers who gain the reputation within their departments for having this type of recorded information soon find that other officers tend to seek them out for suggestions and tips on possible suspects in cases under investigation. The continual recording of bits of information of this kind cannot help but develop the individual officer's overall knowledge of the criminal situation in his assigned area and sometimes within the entire community. It gives him an invaluable insight into recognizing particular modus operandi being used. This is but a natural step to tying particular types of operations to specific suspects.

Checklist for Note-Taking

A primary purpose for including certain points of information in the officer's notebook is to make the officer's testimony less susceptible to successful challenge in court. Obviously, a prerequisite is that the notebook be labeled so that it is clearly identifiable as belonging to a particular officer.

Uniformity of method of recording information in the notebook not only indicates investigative competence by the officer; it also assures that he will not inadvertently fail to record a particular detail that may later prove pertinent. Abbreviations are usually acceptable so long as the officer is consistent in the manner in which he uses them. Rather than continually referring to the complainant or victim by name, both time and space can be saved by identifying the complainant as "C" and the victim as "V." Similarly the suspect can be identified as "S" or in the case or more than one suspect, "S-1," "S-2," and so on. It is important, however, that in cases where the identity of any of these persons is known to the officer at the time he is recording the information, his initial reference should fully identify the person and only in subsequent references should they be referred to by code or abbreviation.

Overall, the recorded information should be understandable and concise and should convey the intended information without indicating a prejudice or bias. In most instances, if the officer has answered the questions who, what, why, when, where, and how, he has recorded the pertinent information.

An additional point worth the officer's consideration is that he should make a particular effort to identify the persons he interviewed or attempted to interview who were uncooperative or who were negative witnesses. Such information can be as important as identifying those persons who did claim to have relevant information. On occasion, individuals have told an officer at the scene of an offense that they had no knowledge of the incident and later appeared in court and testified for the defense in great detail about what took place. Obviously, if the officer can refer to his notes and state that the individual had previously denied any such knowledge, his statement will help impeach the witness's testimony.

Descriptions of Persons and Property

Two basic forms of description are used in submitting written descriptions of individuals and on occasion the two forms are combined into one. The general description, which is used in conjunction with the identity of the complainant or victim or of suspects, consists of the person's name and/or nickname, his sex, race, and age (including birth date if obtainable). When a more detailed description is needed, specific points of description are added. These include the person's known or apparent height, weight, hair color and type, color of eyes, complexion, and any physical marks, scars, or deformities (including tattoos, birthmarks, and abnormalities such as six fingers or toes).

In describing property, the reporting officer should remember that the key to describing a piece of property for later identification or recognition is to describe it in such a way that a person reading the description could pick that particular article from among other similar articles or could recognize it from the description. Rather than describing a stolen ring as a "man's gold wedding ring," a conscientious officer would try to provide a more complete description: "Man's gold wedding ring, gold color, with engraved lines forming a series of diamond-shaped squares. Engraved initials G.P. on underside."

In residential burglaries thieves often take clothing. While they may remove all identifying labels from the clothes, particularly if they intend to resell them, various identification marks are available with which to identify a particular piece of clothing. In the case of a man's suit, after detailed questioning of the owner, an officer could probably compile a description similar to the following: "Man's double-breasted business suit, pin-striped, medium gray with darker gray stripes. Brand name Bonds. Size 46 medium. No cuffs, and pants have been lengthened. Right inside breast pocket has several red ink stains on outside. Right pants leg has been rewoven at area of knee due to cigarette burn."

With effort and attention to detail it is usually possible to provide a description sufficiently distinctive so as to make possible the later identification of the article. A description similar to the example above—"man's gold wedding ring"—merely serves to reinforce the old axiom that anything worth doing is worth doing well.

CHAPTER 6

Laws
of Arrest

The limitations embodied in our Constitution require that law enforcement officers have reasonable or probable cause before arresting any person. The Fourth Amendment to the Constitution further provides:

> The right of the people to be secure in their persons, houses, papers, and effects, against unreasonable searches and seizures, shall not be violated, and no warrants shall issue, but upon reasonable cause, supported upon oath or affirmation, and particularly describing the place to be searched, and the persons or things to be seized.

Generally defined, the Fourth Amendment specifies that a police officer, in order to make a lawful arrest, must have sufficient information that would lead a reasonable person to believe that the person to be arrested had committed a crime. Similarly, the probable cause standard defines the dimensions within which a police officer is expected to base his decision to make an arrest. Probable cause is generally defined as "facts or apparent facts, viewed through the eyes of the experienced police officer, which would generate a reasonable belief that a crime has been committed."

Felonies and Misdemeanors

Basically, an arrest is the taking of a person into custody for reasons and in a manner prescribed by law. While each crime for which an individual can be arrested falls either into the category of felony or into that of misdemeanor, the distinction that various jurisdictions draw between a felony and a misdemeanor is somewhat arbitrary.

A very general guideline that is useful in differentiating the two categories is that any offense punishable by a fine or a penalty of up to one year's confinement is a misdemeanor, and any offense punishable by more than one year in custody is a felony. In the case of a felony offense, it is not required that a police officer actually witness the offense in order to make a legal arrest. He need only have reasonable cause to believe that the suspect either committed or was about to commit a felony. In the case of a misdemeanor offense, on the other hand, it is necessary for the officer to witness the offense before he can make an arrest.

Misdemeanor offenses generally include such crimes as public drunkenness, gambling, prostitution, vagrancy, and disturbing the peace. In offenses of this type, as with practically all "victimless" crimes, the police officer is deemed to be acting for the good of the community when he observes the violations and makes an arrest *based upon his personal observations.*

In some instances criminal acts that are defined as felonies in one jurisdiction will be classified as misdemeanors in another. Purse-snatching is classified as strong-arm or unarmed robbery in some jurisdictions. In others, it is recognized as theft. In jurisdictions where it is classified as theft, the determination as to whether it will be classified as a felony theft or a misdemeanor theft—sometimes called grand theft or petty theft—is based on the amount of money or property involved.

As an example, under one jurisdictional criminal code, grand theft involves amounts of at least one hundred dollars; otherwise, the crime is classified as a petty theft—a misdemeanor. If the loss is in valuable property rather than money, the same jurisdiction divides felony grand theft from misdemeanor petty theft at fifty dollars. By using this interpretation, if a victim had her purse snatched, and it contained $90 in cash and a piece of jewelry at $20, the total value of the loss would be $110, classifying the purse snatch as grand theft, a felony. In a jurisdiction where purse-snatching is classified as robbery rather than theft, the offense is a felony regardless of the amount of the loss. Even if the victim's purse contained no valuables, the act of taking it from her forcibly would constitute robbery, a felony.

The "reasonable cause" doctrine that is used to justify an action or an arrest by a police officer in a felony situation is basically simple yet seldom fully understood. As mentioned, under certain circumstances a police officer can arrest a person he believes has committed or is about to commit a felony offense. The officer may even kill the suspect and be justified in his actions, even if it is later determined that no crime had been committed or attempted.

The justification or reasonableness of the officer's actions is judged by applying the reasonable cause doctrine. This simply means that if a reasonable and prudent person had available to him the same information available to the officer *at the time he acted*, and if this information would have caused a reasonable and prudent person to draw the same conclusions or take the same action the officer took, then the officer's actions were justified *because he acted reasonably.*

As an example, a few years ago a police officer stopped a person on a poorly lit, quiet street, late at night. At the time he got out of his police car to approach the suspect, the officer ordered the man not to move. Instead, the suspect reached into his pocket and withdrew what appeared to be a metal object, and what the officer believed to be a gun. The officer immediately drew his gun and fired, killing the suspect. It was later determined that the suspect was a deaf-mute and that the "weapon" he withdrew from his pocket was a plastic card identifying him as such.

Although no crime had been committed by the suspect, and

although the evidence indicated that he could not have heard the officer's instructions to remain still, the grand jury that investigated the shooting ruled that the officer had acted in a reasonable manner by killing the suspect when he assumed that his own life was in danger. In essence, the jurors indicated that they believed that had they been in the officer's position and had available to them the same information the officer had at that time, they would have acted in a similar manner.

Citizen's Arrest

A lawful arrest by a police officer must embody, to some degree, intent, authority, seizure or restraint, and understanding. In the case of an arrest of a citizen by another citizen, however, there is no law that requires the suspect or accused person to submit to authority, and the seizure or restraint by the citizen making the arrest must be actual, whereas in the case of a police officer the restraint may be either actual or constructive (implied). A police officer merely informing a suspect that he is under arrest constitutes restraint. Basically, in any arrest by a citizen, the arresting citizen must be able to detain the suspect physically, but the suspect is not required by law to submit peacefully to such an arrest. In addition, whereas a police officer may make a felony arrest on the basis of reasonable cause, in the case of a felony arrest by a citizen, the arresting citizen must have actually witnessed the offense, since he can be held in both civil and criminal jeopardy for arresting an innocent person.

Use of Deadly and Necessary Force

A police officer, when acting lawfully, is authorized to use all necessary force to accomplish an arrest. Whether the crime for which an individual is being arrested is minor or serious has no bearing on the officer's right to overcome any resistance in effecting the arrest.

Most jurisdictions have laws that require the citizen to submit to an officer's arrest regardless of whether the citizen was guilty of the crime for which he is being arrested. The rationale behind this statutory provision is that as long as the officer is acting reasonably and has reasonable cause at the time of the arrest, he should not be burdened by a law that allows the person being arrested to resist on the grounds that he is innocent of a crime. If such resistance were permissible, it is entirely possible that it would be to the advantage of the person being arrested to use deadly force in his resistance as a means of eliminating the only individual who would have been a witness connecting him with a criminal offense.

By a continuation of this same reasoning it is held that merely because a defendant is later ruled innocent at a trial after being arrested, it does not necessarily follow that the arresting officer is civilly liable for false arrest. Again, the pivotal question would be—did the officer have reasonable cause *at the time of the arrest?* Again, the most generally accepted interpretation of reasonable cause is whether, based on the information available to the officer at the time, a reasonable and prudent person in the officer's position would have acted similarly.

The necessary force needed to complete an arrest should not be confused with deadly force. That is to say, the force that is needed to subdue a person who is resisting—but not attempting to kill or inflict great bodily harm on the officer—is not intended to include lethal force. Deadly or lethal force should be considered a last resort and is justified only under specific conditions. It is not enough, however, to examine only the legal justification for the use of deadly force by a police officer. The question of the value of a human life must of necessity enter any discussion of the use of deadly force.

Legally, most jurisdictions hold that a police officer is justified in shooting to kill when he is defending his own life or the life of some other person, or as a last resort in capturing a fleeing felon. As to the justification in defending his life, if the officer has reason to believe his life is threatened, or that he is in danger of great bodily harm, he is justified in killing his attacker. Similarly, if he is defending some other person's life, or is defending that person from great bodily harm, *and the threat is immediate,* his use of lethal force would be justified.

The word *immediate* is an important part of the justification of his act. A necessary factor in establishing the justification for self-defense or the defense of another person is that the attacker must have, at the time he makes a threat or a preliminary move to carry out his threat, the ability to accomplish the act. Claims of self-defense have been denied by courts on this point. If, for example, a suspect told the victim that the next time he saw him he was going to kill him, the court would very probably rule that this did not constitute an immediate threat to the victim's life. Similarly, if the suspect stated that he was going home to get a gun with which to kill the victim, such a statement would not only establish that the threat to the victim's life was not immediate, but it would also indicate that the time of the threat the suspect did not possess the means to carry it out. Furthermore, when the suspect stated that he was going home to get his gun, the intended victim only needed to leave the scene during the suspect's absence as a means of protecting himself.

The moral question of when a police officer is justified in taking a person's life is much more difficult and sensitive. The possibility of killing an innocent person, a person who was later found to be unarmed, or a juvenile is always present. Unlike an arrest, where a defendant later has the opportunity to prove his innocence and gain his freedom, a killing is irrevocable. It is precisely because the police officer is empowered to take a person's life that he would continually keep in mind his obligation to weigh the necessity of taking a life. Simply the fact that a person is a fleeing felon does not necessarily mean he should be killed. In any circumstance the value of a human life must be weighed against the right to take a life. As with so many of the problems a police officer must face, his decision in such a case must be nearly instantaneous.

The Rights of the Accused

The rights of a person accused of a criminal offense are summed up by the Fifth Amendment to the Constitution:

No person shall be held to answer for a capital, or otherwise infamous crime, unless on a presentment or indictment of a Grand Jury, except in cases arising in the land or naval forces, or in the Militia, when in actual service in time of War or public danger; Nor shall any person be subject for the same offense to be twice put in jeopardy of life or limb; nor shall be compelled in any criminal case to be a witness against himself, nor be deprived of life, liberty or property, without due process of law; nor shall private property be taken for public use, without just compensation.

Insofar as the police officer is concerned, the Fifth Amendment is most commonly related to the right of the accused to remain silent and not be compelled to answer questions. As a result of the case of *Miranda* v. *Arizona*, the Supreme Court further defined the breadth of the Fifth Amendment. The court ruled that the Fifth Amendment holds outside of criminal court proceedings and serves to protect persons whether or not they have actually been arrested. The court stated that a person suspected or accused of a crime must be adequately and effectively apprised of his right to remain silent, and his exercise of that right must be recognized and honored.

The court made clear that at the very outset, a person in custody must first be informed in clear and unequivocal terms that he has the right to remain silent. This warning must be accompanied by an explanation that anything said by the accused can and will be used against him in court. One of the more standard forms by which a suspect is admonished and advised of his constitutional rights is the following statement, which is usually read by the police officer to the suspect:

> You have the right to remain silent and to refuse to give any written or oral statement. You have the right to be represented by an attorney. Anything you say can and will be used against you.

The overall intent of these requirements is that the accused be aware of the consequences of answering questions so that he can fully understand his rights and make intelligent use of his right to avoid self-incrimination.

Another point of importance to the police officer is that once the accused has indicated that he is unwilling to answer any interrogations, all questioning of him must cease.

Search and Seizure

The Fourth Amendment, quoted at the beginning of the chapter, deals with the sensitive area of search and seizure. Of importance to the police officer is a vital exception to this rule against search and seizure—that is, search incident to a lawful arrest. In practice, the great majority of searches are incident to an arrest rather than under a warrant.

The law permits an arresting officer to conduct a search of a person who has been taken into custody for concealed weapons and for a means by which to effect an escape. Additionally, such a search is permitted as a means of preventing the destruction of any evidence the arrested person may possess.

The ultimate justification for searches incident to lawful arrest and without a search warrant is that the arrest precede the search. The search is *not* a justification for the arrest. As with all rules, however, this one has its exception.

The guidelines outlining the justification for stopping and frisking a suspect name certain circumstances in which the officer is permitted to question and frisk a person without having first placed him under arrest. The present interpretation of stop and frisk is based on the U.S. Supreme Court's ruling in *Terry* v. *Ohio.* In addressing itself to that particular case, the court rejected the theory that the search under discussion was incident to a lawful arrest, but ruled instead that the officer, based on his experience, had reasonable cause to conclude that the defendants were acting suspiciously and that some interrogation of them was warranted. The court held further that, purely for his own protection, the officer was justified in patting down the outer clothing of the suspect. The court then distinguished between an investigatory "stop" and an arrest, and a "frisk" of the outer clothing for weapons as opposed to a full-blown search for evidence of crime. Under these circumstances, the illegal weapons the officer discovered as a result of frisking the suspects were justification for their subsequent arrest.

This ruling of the Supreme Court affirmed the decision of the Court of Appeals for the Eighth Judicial District of Ohio, which had upheld the suspects' convictions in superior court. Again, this decision underlines the necessity for police officers to make nearly instantaneous decisions that meet the criterion of reasonableness that others determine at their leisure.

Admonishing the Suspect

The police officer's responsibility to admonish the suspect is based, as was stated earlier, on the Supreme Court's ruling in the case of *Miranda* v. *Arizona.*

From the point of view of the police officer, the importance of the *Miranda* ruling is not only that the accused has certain specified rights, but that he must be made aware of his rights. In subsequent rulings, it has been held that it is the responsibility of the police, before they begin any interrogation of the suspect, to advise him that he is a suspect and to notify him of his right to remain silent and to be represented by an attorney.

Some police departments have the suspect sign a statement acknowledging that he has been informed of his constitutional rights. A common practice is to have the statement advising the suspect of his rights printed on the official arrest report. Usually it is at the top of the space used for the narrative part of the report. The statement, usually of a form identical or similar to that mentioned earlier in this chapter, is also signed by the officer who read it to the suspect, and the date and time it was read is also entered in the report.

The police officer should be aware, however, that merely reading such a statement to a suspect does not necessarily guarantee that all the suspect's rights have been protected. In the *Miranda* case the Supreme Court held that even though the defendant had signed a statement admitting "full knowledge" of his legal rights, this did not necessarily constitute an intelligent waiver of these rights. While this is an area still under challenge and litigation, its basic intent is to insure that in addition to having his legal rights read or recited to him, the suspect should be made to understand that he is not under threat or pressure nor in danger of recrimination from the officers if he should choose to take advantage of his rights and refuse to answer any questions. The aim of this ruling is that the suspect not only should be told his rights but must understand them fully, since only with full understanding can he make an intelligent waiver of those rights.

The Officer's Right to Require Identification

Field interrogation and the right to demand that a person adequately identify himself are important tools to the police officer. In the face of the *Miranda* decision, officers have understandably been unsure of their right to continue these practices. Under *Miranda*, however, it was stated that "general on-the-scene questioning as to facts surrounding a crime or other general questioning of citizens in the fact-finding process is not affected."

Generally, the courts have held that as long as no special coercive tactics are used during a field stop, no *Miranda*-type warning is required. A demand by an officer that a person produce identification could, however, be interpreted as coercion. The primary ruling establishing the officer's right to demand identification comes from *Terry* v. *Ohio* and is generally looked upon as the justification for a stop and frisk.

In order to justify his right to frisk a suspect and to demand that the person produce identification, the officer must have reasonable cause to suspect the individual, and a subsequent frisk and demand for identification must be based on the reasonable belief that potential harm exists for the officer or some other person.

Stated simply, if the officer has reasonable cause to believe that the subject has committed or is about to commit a crime, or that the subject poses a present physical threat to some person, the officer can justifiably demand identification. Additionally, many jurisdictions have enacted statutory provisions that make it a criminal offense to refuse to produce identification upon the demand of a police officer.

Recommended Readings

J. Shane Creamer, *The Law of Arrest, Search and Seizure* (W. B. Saunders, Philadelphia, 1968).

CHAPTER 7

Field
Interrogation

Field interrogation has three primary purposes. The narrow view of field interrogation is that it involves only the questioning of persons of whom the officer is suspicious or whom he views as suspects in a criminal offense. There is a much wider use of field interrogation, however, and its effective application is a valuable tool to the patrol officer. Many times such interrogation involves the obtaining of information from persons on the officer's beat, who, although they may be either willing or unwilling to cooperate, possess knowledge that is essential to the officer. Successful interrogation under such circumstances is a valuable skill that usually requires considerable time and application to develop.

It follows, therefore, that the first purpose of field interrogation is to develop information from persons the officer comes in contact with. This will include, but not be limited to, business people, working people, local "characters," suspected criminals, and regular residents or hangers-on in the area.

A second purpose of field interrogation is to obtain identification of persons, many times without their becoming aware that the officer has more than a passing interest in them. Particularly in this type of interrogation it is essential that the officer proceed slowly without seeming to pressure the person or appearing to be officious. Sometimes the officer may find it to his advantage to back off and give the appearance of dropping his interest if he feels that the person being questioned is becoming suspicious or resistant.

Third, interrogation is an invaluable tool when the officer is reporting a crime and conducting the preliminary investigation. This type of interrogation includes obtaining as many names as possible of both suspects and witnesses. Since some individuals volunteer information solely because they want to seem important or to call attention to themselves, any interrogation that serves to eliminate those persons as sources of valid information can be immensely time-saving to the follow-up investigators.

The more widely recognized type of field interrogation involves the officer, on his own volition and based on his own suspicions, stopping persons when he has less than reasonable cause on which to base an arrest and questioning them as to their identity, address, employment, and so on. In this type of interrogation, much is left to the individual officer's discretion, and the lack of discretion or recognition of the individual's rights may well prove a bar to future prosecution.

In many departments this type of field interrogation is recorded on a computer-type card furnished specifically for that purpose. These cards usually request, in addition to the person's name and address, such information as the person's age and birthdate, his physical description and dress, the location of the stop, whether the person was in a car and if so its description, and the identities of any persons in the company of the person being questioned. One of the drawbacks to the use of this type of field interrogation card is that it seems to encourage many officers subconsciously to make excessive use of their own personal racial or class prejudices in determining that certain individuals or groups appear suspicious to them. Some officers are prone to view a black person as suspicious in situations where, if the person had been white, no suspicion would have been aroused. This seems to be particularly true of officers who tend to stop for questioning black persons driving expensive autos. Similarly, some officers tend to concentrate their field interrogation efforts on hippie-type persons with long hair. While this problem is not as prevalent it was five or six years ago, many white police officers still tend to be politically conservative, with a pronouned bias against persons they identify as "left-wingers." A field interrogation made on this kind of basis poses the possibility that further legal restrictions will be placed on the police officer's ability to question people.

For an officer to be able to conduct field interrogations successfully he must have discretion, skill, and knowledge. Knowledge of up-to-date rulings as to individual rights is a must, and the officer's knowledge of what constitutes reasonable cause may in the end be the determining factor in judging whether he was justified in an interrogation. Discretion and skill are all-important in questioning people. Different approaches fit different situations just as they fit different people.

In the following example of good interrogation of a suspect by an officer, note how many times the suspect commits himself to specific points without being questioned in detail about these points by the officer:

OFFICER: Have you been in the pool hall long?

SUSPECT: No, I just came down here a while ago with Willie. He picked me up at home, and we drove around a while, then came by here.

OFFICER: Did you and Willie talk to anyone before you got here?

SUSPECT: Well, we stopped by my woman's pad for a couple of minutes, but that was all.

With only a few general questions, the officer has the suspect committed to a specific story that can be checked out in detail. First, the obvious alibi witness is Willie. According to the suspect, Willie has a car that can be checked (for description, if the suspected crime involved an auto). The suspect claims to have spent his entire time between leaving home and arriving at the pool hall with Willie, a point that can be checked by questioning the suspect's girlfriend. The location of the girlfriend's home could also be relevant to the suspected crime.

In this kind of interrogation, it is to the officer's advantage not to challenge or appear to doubt the suspect's story. A person who has reason to attempt to cover up his movements will tend to expand any lies he tells the officer when he feels the officer believes him. The more the suspect lies, the more ammunition the officer has with which to confront him later. While some officers view being lied to as a challenge to their authority, it is often the best course to let a person lie without acknowledging disbelief. In some investigative situations it can be as important to pin the suspect down to a lie as to get him to tell the truth. In any event, getting a person to furnish any information, regardless of its veracity, is a positive step in any investigation and is considerably better than having him refuse to answer any questions. Untruthful answers can be used later to pressure the individual to answer further questions more truthfully.

It almost goes without saying that the same approach cannot be used in all instances. The officer must first judge the type of person he is dealing with before making any attempt to question the individual. Even then, during the course of the questioning he may well have to reevaluate his judgment and at the same time reevaluate the person's responses.

Differences between Interrogation and Interview

An officer conducting an *interview* of a possible witness to a criminal offense has a different purpose from that of the officer who is conducting an *interrogation*. The primary purpose of the interview is to learn what information, if any, the witness has and to extract it from him in such a way as to separate opinion from fact. In an interrogation, the officer is more likely to use guile while still endeavoring to obtain information. He may want the suspect to believe he knows more than he actually does; he may imply—sometimes by advising the suspect of his rights—that the suspect is about to be arrested if he does not tell the truth.

With witnesses the officer often must be more subtle and tactful. He must persuade the witness to want to cooperate. This is often easier said than done. Some potential witnesses are reluctant to become involved, while others either are overly willing to cooperate and volunteer more information than they actually have, or are attempting to play detective and give observations tainted by their own analysis of the situation. Other witnesses are easily influenced by the remarks or observations of others and tend to make their observations conform to what they have heard others state. As a result, a witness sometimes unintentionally furnishes false information to the officer. The witness may be highly emotional as a result of the crime he observed, and while it may in a sense seem cruel, it may be that the officer can obtain more accurate and detailed information from this witness at that time rather than waiting for him to regain his composure.

When the officer is interrogating orally or taking a written statement during an interrogation, he should generally make a particular effort to note or record the actual words of the person being questioned. The officer's testimony or the statement he recorded may be ruled inadmissible in court if the wording does not accurately reflect the statements of the person he interrogated. In some instances the statement has been ruled inadmissible because the wording used included phrases or terminology that was unknown to the witness or suspect. Other statements have been ruled inadmissible because the wording used included specific legal or professional terms that in all probability would only be used by a police officer.

For example, in one case the defendant had supposedly given an officer a statement in which he acknowledged his awareness of his constitutional right to refuse to answer questions. The suspect was a nearly illiterate farm worker, and the statement that was attributed to him by the officer said in part, "I thoroughly understand the context of the Fifth Amendment wherein I have the right to remain silent." In all fairness, the court could not believe that an uneducated person would have made such a technically correct and legal statement.

In addition to his responsibility to accurately quote persons he has questioned, the officer has the responsibility during questioning to narrow the scope of the subject and press the person being questioned to be as accurate as possible. In this kind of questioning it is justifiable and proper for the officer to attempt to help the witness recall his observations, but without coaching the witness. For example, if a witness were attempting to provide a physical description of a suspect, the officer could ask the witness to compare the suspect's height to that of the officer and to judge whether the suspect was taller, shorter, or the same height.

It is generally recognized that teen-age boys are particularly good witnesses in describing automobiles. Girls, on the other hand, are often poor witnesses when describing anything other than the clothing of other persons in their own age group. While many witnesses are vague in estimating the height of others, young children are particularly likely to overestimate the height of adults. An officer attempting to get a physical description of a suspect (height, weight, hair color, age, and so on) from a child can often come up with a fairly accurate description by having the witness make comparisons for all of these characteristics with some other person. If the witness should state that a suspect was five feet ten and weighed about 170 pounds, the officer should check the accuracy of the observations by having the witness estimate the officer's height and weight. Similarly, the officer can often ask the witness to estimate the officer's age or to compare his age to that of the suspect. In general, witnesses are most likely to be weak or inaccurate in their descriptions of persons of other races. Adult women are generally good witnesses in describing other adults of the same race—particularly other women and their clothing. Older men, perhaps because they spend more time merely watching others and are less likely to be distracted than are younger people, are often good witnesses when it comes to describing an overall scene, especially in identifying how many persons were involved in an incident, and in identifying other potential witnesses.

To summarize the primary differences between an interrogation and an interview: an interrogation, which is likely to come up at a later date in court, should be based on exactly what the witness or suspect stated, and his own words should be recorded. Such a statement is often used as a means of committing the person giving it to a specific story or alibi. An interview, on the other hand, should be conducted to gain all the information possible, and the investigating officer should use whatever means are at his disposal to help the person being interviewed furnish accurate information.

Techniques of Interrogation

An officer intending to interrogate a possible suspect should first be sure he is prepared. He should have all the information that is available before he begins any questioning. In a good interrogation the officer tries to encourage the suspect to talk voluntarily and to establish whether the suspect is answering questions truthfully. As mentioned before, one means by which this goal is sometimes achieved is by the officer impressing on the person being questioned that he believes the person's statements (whether or not he actually does) in order to get the individual to talk more freely. When individuals are encouraged to talk freely they tend to contradict themselves on any points that are not truthful. In some instances, even though the person under questioning has given false information, his information tends to implicate him to the extent that it can be used as a lever to get the truth from him at a later date.

Some officers tend to have quicker minds than others when it comes to assessing the suspect's story on the spot. Sometimes the officer can trip up the suspect each time he gives false information. As long as the officer is sure of his ground he may in this way be able to make the suspect give more accurate information because he believes that the officer knows all the details anyway. This, however, is a game of bluffing that if overdone can cause a loss of information to the officer. The practice of challenging a suspect each time the officer merely suspects that he is being untruthful runs a greater risk of terminating an interrogation than it does of producing useful information.

Written Statements and Confessions

In all probability there will be many occasions on which the patrol officer will have the opportunity or the duty to record a statement or a confession. In addition to his knowing the legal framework within which such a statement is acceptable, it is necessary for him to understand the legal differences between a *confession* and an *admission*.

Basically, in addition to being an admission of responsibility for a criminal act, a confession will include a statement that the act was done with the intention of committing a crime. By comparison, an admission will acknowledge responsibility for the act without acknowledging or admitting the element of criminal intent. While the statements in the admission may tend to incriminate the person making them, if the statement does not specifically acknowledge criminal intent, it cannot be identified as a confession.

The full understanding by the patrol officer of these legal technicalities can help him in his questioning of a suspect. He will be aware that the information he is attempting to gain from the suspect falls into one of these two categories, and the question of whether or not the suspect gives a written confession may well depend on the officer's skill and knowledge.

The primary prerequisite for any written confession or statement taken by the officer is that it was given freely and voluntarily. Again, the determination of whether such a statement was actually given freely and voluntarily is based on legal outlines, and the statement must satisfy these outlines in order to be acceptable in court. While it is not absolutely mandatory, such statements whenever possible *should be in the suspect's own handwriting*. If this is not practical, the police officer can record the statement exactly as given to him by the suspect and then have the suspect first read it aloud and then sign it. If at all possible, there should be another person present who can sign that he or she witnessed the giving of the statement.

Before the officer attempts to take any such statement from a suspect, however, whether the statement be oral or written, the suspect must be advised of his constitutional right to refuse to give the statement and to refuse to make any statement or give any information to the officer.

It is a careless and sometimes dangerous practice for the officer to merely read a prepared statement to the suspect, outlining his constitutional rights, and then ask the suspect if he understands his rights. When the suspect has been admonished in this manner, some courts have held that this does not constitute intelligent acknowledgment by the suspect that he fully understood his rights at that time.

Rather than reading such a prepared statement to the suspect, the officer is on much firmer legal ground if he advises the suspect verbally and in person that the suspect has the right to remain silent, that any statements he does give can be used against him, and that his decision to remain silent will not and cannot be used against him.

It is the officer's responsibility, therefore, to ascertain that any statement the suspect gives him not only will be free and voluntary but also will be based on the suspect's intelligent understanding of his rights. The statement must reflect this intelligent decision by the suspect to the degree that it will be accepted in court.

The beginning of any such written statement must include the name of the officer taking the statement, where the taking of the statement occurred and the time it occurred, and the names of all persons present during the recording of the statement. Even when the statement is written by the suspect, the possibility exists that due to coaching by the officer the suspect will use phrases or terminology that he picked up from the officer and that are foreign to his manner of speaking. Some "con wise" suspects may even do this deliberately, knowing that they may be able to have the statement ruled inadmissible on the grounds that it was not a true representation of what they had said.

Whatever terms the suspect uses in his own statement should be recorded accurately. If the suspect curses during the statement, the officer should record it. If he uses some type of ethnic or street slang, the officer records it. If the suspect is writing his own statement and does not know how to spell a particular word, the officer should tell him to spell the word in whatever way seems correct to him.

The officer should keep in mind that his overall aim is to obtain a free and voluntary statement, in the suspect's own words, that commits the suspect to a specific alibi or story or that contains a confession or an admission of his participation in a criminal act.

Recommended Reading

Fred E. Inbau and James R. Thompson, *Criminal Law and Its Administration* (Mineola, N.Y.: Foundation Press, 1970), chapter 12, "Interrogations and Confessions."

CHAPTER 8

Street Stops
of Suspects
and Cars

In performing his job the police officer must stop suspects on the street or in automobiles. Sometimes such stops are routine and uneventful, and the person being stopped is cooperative and does not resist. At other times, however, street stops can be potentially dangerous for the officer. He must then first decide whether to stop the person at all and, second, know how to handle the situation in such a way as to reduce risks to his personal safety.

High-Speed Chase

Before undertaking a high-speed chase the patrol officer should evaluate for himself whether the risks involved in such a chase are justified by its purpose. Too often a high-speed chase involves something as minor as a traffic violation, and in some instances the police officer had only a suspicion that the driver of the auto must have committed some offense because he fled from the officer.

The risks involved in high-speed driving, particularly in densely populated areas, are so great that it should be avoided whenever there is any alternative means of stopping or identifying the suspected auto.

An officer chasing a suspect involved in a criminal offense at high speed should keep in mind that his primary aim is to keep the suspect in sight so he can broadcast his location and the direction of flight. Seldom can one police car force a suspect auto to stop unless the car has an accident. As long as the officer giving chase is able to furnish other cars with the suspect car's location and direction, the chances of apprehending the suspect are greatly increased.

If the police car has an accident, the chances of the suspect's escaping are greatly increased. In addition, if the accident damages someone else's auto or property or injures or kills an innocent party, it becomes difficult to justify the officer's actions.

While some officers rationalize that in certain instances, and in the interest of public safety, a wanted person must be apprehended at any cost, the officer making the decision as to whether the risk is justified should apply the same standard in weighing the alternatives as he would in deciding whether to fire his revolver in a situation where innocent bystanders would be endangered. Additionally, a logical argument can be made that a high-speed chase involves more risks than does shooting at a fleeing suspect. Whenever the officer fires his revolver, the primary danger is that he may accidentally strike a bystander. By comparison, in a high-speed chase, the officer not only has his own actions to be concerned with, but he must consider the possibility that he will cause other cars to have accidents in attempting to get out of his way, and that his chasing the suspect may force that auto to have an accident that will kill or injure innocent parties.

An officer would probably choose to conduct a high-speed chase despite the risks in the case of a person who has already killed someone or a person who has in some manner demonstrated his willingness and intent to kill if not apprehended.

Similarly, from time to time police are faced with a criminal or potential criminal who is mentally deranged and must be taken into custody at any cost and with any methods available.

When the officer does become involved in a high-speed chase, it should be standard operating procedure that he uses his flashing or red lights and his siren. These signals will tend to make other traffic at least aware of the police car's approach and lessen the possibility of an accidental collision. Experienced officers, however, are aware that the use of the siren has a possible negative side effect—it makes it difficult for the officer to hear the siren of any other emergency vehicle that might be approaching the same intersection he is approaching. This is why some officers use their sirens only intermittently, as when approaching heavier traffic or approaching intersections.

Even when using his siren, the officer should be aware that under certain conditions the sound of the siren does not carry over a sufficient distance to give adequate warning. As an example, in a police vehicle traveling 90 miles per hour (135 feet per second), the sound of the siren in front of the speeding vehicle is so negligible as to be practically useless as a warning to vehicles or pedestrians that the police car is approaching.

In attempting to stop a vehicle he has been chasing, the officer should refrain from shooting except in the most extreme instances. If a shot should either puncture a tire on the suspect vehicle or hit the driver, the car is likely to go out of control and become an immediate threat to others.

Television and motion pictures often show police officers chasing a suspected auto and cutting it off or forcing it off the road. This tactic, however, is neither advisable nor practical in the great majority of cases. Usually the officer has the advantage of being able to call for assistance from other units, so his primary responsibility becomes that of keeping the suspect auto in sight. If the officer can pass on to the other police units the car's description and direction, it is very unlikely that the suspect will be able to elude all the units in the area. The longer the chase continues, the less chance the suspect usually has of escaping. One reason for this is that if the suspect continues to flee until more than one police unit has him in sight, once he decides to stop his car and flee on foot, his chances of escaping from several officers is slight. If there is more than one person in the suspect auto, it is to the officer's advantage to attempt to get assistance before the car is stopped.

Persons in fleeing cars usually are either "amateurs" who have panicked or persons whose capture will result in more serious charges than they are willing to face. In some cases the suspects' auto will contain evidence that they feel they cannot afford to be caught with.

Once a decision has been made to stop a car forcibly, the techniques to be used should be coordinated among all the police cars involved. Usually the most practical method is to select an area that affords minimal possibility of injury to bystanders and then use a shotgun to shoot out one of the tires on the fleeing auto. If the various police units are aware of the plan of attack, they can position themselves so as not to become involved in a collision with the suspect car and at the same time be prepared to apprehend any suspects who may attempt to flee from the car once it has been brought to a halt.

Car Search

To a degree, the circumstances of the arrest will dictate to the officer how detailed a search of the vehicle he should make. If the driver was arrested for drunk driving, it may be that the only search necessary will be checking the area within reach of the driver immediately before he was stopped by the arresting officer. Such a search would be primarily for the purpose of attempting to locate a container of liquor.

If the car has passengers in addition to the driver and the officer has reason to suspect the commission of a more serious offense, he may need to conduct a more systematic and intensive search. Prior to any search, however, all occupants of the car should be removed. If the officer is working alone and is unable to keep the suspect or suspects safely in custody after removing them from the car, and at the same time conduct a search of the car, he should postpone the search until later. Even if he does not intend to conduct a search of the auto at that time, it is still good police practice to remove all suspects from the car as soon as practicable. The longer the suspects are allowed to remain in the car, the greater the possibility that they will be able to destroy some evidence or gain access to a concealed weapon.

An important consideration at this point is the protection of the chain of evidence. If the arresting officer is unable to conduct a search of the suspect's auto immediately after removing the passengers from it, he should take steps to insure that the car is not tampered with before he does have an opportunity to make a search. Merely locking the car and leaving it at that location with the intent of returning later in order to conduct a search is inadequate. If important evidence were obtained after the officer returned to the locked auto, the court could rule the evidence inadmissible on the grounds that the officer had no way of knowing what other persons had keys to the car and therefore had the ability to remove or plant evidence in it while it was unattended.

In most situations the arresting officer can call for assistance, and after turning over the arrested person to another officer, he can then conduct a search. If it is necessary to take the car into police custody before it is searched, the officer should remain at the scene until official seals have been placed on the doors and trunk of the car and it has been towed away. If placing seals is not practical, the officer must, in order to protect the quality of any potential evidence, follow the tow truck as it takes the suspect auto to the garage. In such an arrangement the officer should be able to testify in court that he kept the tow truck and the car in view at all times and that no one tampered with the car.

When the officer is in the process of stopping an auto, he can sometimes gain a clue as to what area to search first by paying close attention to the driver. Even before a suspect auto has stopped, the driver sometimes will lean far to his right. This can be an indication that he is reaching for the glove compartment or that he is reaching under the right side of the front seat. If there is more than one person in the car, the officer should try to spot suspicious moves on the part of any passenger. The more persons there are in the car, the more possible areas there are where evidence or a weapon could be concealed.

A basic rule for an officer conducting a search of an auto is that his search should be systematic. An officer without a preconceived idea of the nature of the evidence for which he is searching is less likely to overlook something of importance. An officer who is primarily searching for a gun may overlook a matchbook or a folded gum wrapper. Many individuals use matchbooks to record phone numbers or addresses. Often the reason is that the information is confidential and the person wants to be able to dispose of it easily and without arousing suspicion. Investigating officers who take time to look for this kind of evidence and check out the information are often rewarded with valuable clues.

In some investigations the source of the matchbook itself furnishes valuable facts, indicating that the user has patronized the cocktail lounge, hotel, motel, or restaurant advertised on it.

Gum wrappers have been used as containers for illegal narcotics, as betting slips, and as a means of passing information from one person to another. It is basically true that in criminal investigations the most innocent-looking article often can supply the clue that will ultimately lead to the solution of a case.

Any search the officer feels is justified is worth doing well. An officer must constantly guard against a tendency merely to go through the motions of conducting a search. That too many officers do this has been shown time after time when suspects who have been arrested and searched are later found to have a weapon or an article of evidence in their possession. Part of a police officer's job is to be suspicious, and the more suspicious the officer is, the more likely he is to spot incriminating evidence.

Removing Suspects from a Car

Three considerations of primary importance when an officer removes a suspect or suspects from a car are: (1) the safety of the officer, (2) assurance that the suspects are not given an opportunity to escape, and (3) the protection of any evidence in possession of the suspects or under their control.

While many intricate methods are used to preserve and protect evidence, it is of primary importance that the evidence be handled as little as possible and that if at all feasible it be photographed before being handled at all. The officer who originally discovered a piece of evidence should be the person responsible for recovering it, tagging it or marking it for identification, and delivering it to the police property or evidence room. The chain of possession in the handling of potential evidence is all-important in a criminal trial. If a defense attorney is able to gain an admission from an officer that he was careless in handling a piece of evidence, or if that evidence cannot be accounted for by police records continuously from time of recovery to the time it is presented in court, the admissibility of the evidence in court is seriously threatened.

If there is only one suspect in the stopped car, the officer usually should get him out as soon as possible. While it is not practical in all instances for the officer to approach the stopped auto with his revolver in his hand, neither should he approach the car without being prepared to defend himself instantly. Whenever possible, an officer should approach from the driver's left rear so that if the driver should attempt to attack the officer or shoot at him, he will have to turn around in the seat, a move that would be easily seen, giving the officer an opportunity to act or to take cover. If the officer approaches from the driver's front, he has no way of knowing whether the driver is intending to fire at him and has no warning since the driver would be able to sit in a normal position with his hands out of the officer's sight.

The reason for approaching from the driver's left side is again for the officer's protection. By standing on the left side just behind the seated driver, the officer again puts the suspect in the position of having to make a very noticeable and unnatural move in order to attack. In addition, the officer is in a position to open the car door and better observe the suspect and keep his hands in sight.

Sometimes an experienced officer, after stopping a car with the intention of questioning or searching the occupants, decides upon approaching the car to change his tactics. A lone officer must evaluate the situation and decide instantly whether he can successfully remove the suspects from the auto, arrest and search them, and search the auto. In some cases he decides that he cannot accomplish these tasks without a risk to himself that outweighs his probability of success. The quick-thinking officer will then attempt to put the occupants of the car at ease by saying that his purpose in stopping them was to warn the driver that he had committed some minor violation or to tell him of some equipment deficiency on the auto.

If the officer feels he can thus reassure the occupants of the car and let them go after having the driver produce identification, he has gained potentially valuable information—the driver's identity and a good look at the passengers. In any event the officer has bought himself additional time, and after letting the suspects drive off, he can take steps to call in other officers to assist him in making a successful stop of the suspect auto.

Once the officer has decided to remove the suspect or suspects from the car, the assumption is that he has legal grounds for an arrest. Therefore, he is in the position of ordering the suspects to obey his orders and demanding their compliance. Particularly when there is more than one suspect in the car, the officer needs to be firm and to demand instant response to his orders. Often the officer will have his revolver drawn, so his situation is somewhat complicated. As much as possible, he will want to stay out of arm's reach of the suspects while at the same time keeping them as fully in view as possible as they exit from the car. Under no circumstances should the officer let any of the suspects exit from the right side of the car. It is vitally important, for the officer's own protection, that he have all suspects come out on the side of the car where he is standing. As each suspect exits, he should be ordered to assume the spread-eagle position, facing the left side of the car. In demanding that each suspect in turn take this position, with his feet as far apart as possible and with his hands on the hood or top of the car, the officer has minimized the suspects' ability to jump him with a surprise attack. By ordering the suspects to move their feet back away from the car as much as four to five feet, the officer has placed them in such an off-balance position that he will have a maximum of control over their movements. Except in cases where there is no alternative, the lone officer should not attempt to go any further in searching or handcuffing the suspects or searching the auto. These things can be done much more safely and efficiently when the officer has been joined by reinforcements.

When more than one suspect is lined up against the side of the car, they can be safely handcuffed together. Assuming that the officer is holding his revolver in his right hand, he should first order the suspect standing nearest the front of the car to put his left hand behind his back while still maintaining his position.

Using his left hand, the officer can then place one handcuff on the suspect's left wrist. The second suspect is then ordered to put his left hand behind the back of the first suspect and the two men are handcuffed together, both by their left wrists.

The advantage to handcuffing the suspects together by their left wrists is that they are thus unable to face the officer at the same time if they attempt resistance. On the other hand, if two suspects were handcuffed left wrist to right wrist, they could very effectively attack and subdue a single officer and flee. Even though being handcuffed together would be somewhat of a disadvantage, it would not appreciably decrease their ability to run.

Legality of the Car Search

Basically, the law provides that the police officer may search a suspect after he has been arrested if the search is incident to the arrest. Among the technicalities of this ruling is the fact that the search *cannot* be conducted if it is *not* incident to the arrest. For example, if an officer arrested a person for a minor traffic offense and had no reason to suspect any other crime or to suspect that the person had any illegal evidence in his possession, a search following the arrest would be prohibited.

In a case in which a search of the arrested person is justified, it is generally recognized that both the suspect's person and the areas under his control are subject to search. Thus, if the suspect were either the operator of or a passenger in a car at the time of his arrest, and if the circumstances of the arrest justified a search of his person, then the same circumstances would justify a search of the inside of the auto. This can be true even in certain types of driving violations. If the arrest charged intoxication while operating the auto, a search for liquor as evidence to back up the charge would then be justifiable. If the search revealed other evidence, unrelated to the arrest charge, such evidence would also be legal.

The courts have expressed differing views on the legality of a search incident to an arrest and without a search warrant that included the locked trunk of an auto. One view is that the locked trunk is not an area immediately accessible to the driver or passenger of the car and that such a search should not be conducted without a search warrant. An officer would probably be safe if he attempted to find grounds for towing the car—possibly for safe-keeping—at the time of the arrest, and if probable cause could be developed, he could apply for a search warrant.

From a practical point of view, there is another possible approach to this problem that is sometimes used by experienced officers. The officer can sometimes base his decision on whether to risk a questionable search and the possibility that the evidence he might recover would be ruled inadmissible in court on the use he could make of the evidence. If the officer had no intention of making use of the evidence in court, but rather viewed it as a potential lead to other evidence or to other suspects, he might logically conclude that the risk of having his evidence ruled inadmissible in court was of little consequence.

There is one method by which an officer can search an auto without first arresting the driver or having a search warrant. This is if the driver waives his right to refuse such a search. This waiver must be intelligent, however, in that the person giving the officer his permission to conduct the search must know both the implications of the search and that he has the legal right to refuse such a search. Such a waiver must be made intelligently and without pressure or threats on the part of the officer.

Searching and Handcuffing Suspects

An earlier part of this chapter discussed methods for removing suspects from an auto and handcuffing them. In any such search conducted incident to an arrest, the officer's primary concern is to discover whether the suspect has any weapons that could be used against the officer. It is therefore only necessary at this time for the officer to conduct a thorough frisk or outside search of the suspect, paying particular attention to areas in which the suspect might conceal an easily accessible weapon. After such a search, the officer should proceed to handcuff the suspect.

A frisk for weapons should be conducted systematically. Usually it starts at the suspect's shoulders. The officer should run his hands over the suspect's body in such a way that he will feel any lump or foreign object that might be in a pocket or fitted or taped against the suspect's skin. The insides of the arms and the armpits should be closely checked. The officer should run his hands firmly over the suspect's chest, sides, and back. It is usually advisable to check the suspect's waistband by putting the hands inside it and running them completely around the waist.

One of the most popular parts of the body in which to conceal weapons or narcotics is the crotch next to the testicles. It is this area of the body that police officers most often pass over with no real attempt to check thoroughly. The officer should continue to feel down each leg and each ankle for any unusual lumps or bulges. Finally, it is often advisable to remove the suspect's shoes and socks and to check the shoes separately.

Since it is not practical to undress the suspect on the street during a search, the officer will have to rely on feeling the suspect's body through his clothes. He should press firmly with his hands through the clothing, and then slide his hands along rather than patting or moving them from place to place. The officer is much more likely to spot a suspicious bulge or feel something under the clothing if he slides his hands along. While there will be some situations in which the officer will be understandably reluctant to use his bare hands in conducting a search of a suspect, he should remember that if the search is worth doing at all, it is worth doing right. An officer who attempts to conduct such a search with his gloves on is far less likely to spot a suspicious bulge in or under the suspect's clothing. And the greater the lapse of time before an efficient search is made, the greater the possibility that the suspect will have an opportunity to dispose of potential evidence against him.

While the wall search is the most common, the officer may sometimes have the suspect lie prone, face down, while being searched. The officer must then have the suspect roll over so that both the front and back of the body can be frisked thoroughly. When the prone position is to be used, the officer should cuff the suspect's hands behind his back before conducting the search.

While handcuffing a suspect, the officer should always attempt to keep him in as awkward a position as possible. The wall search position is practical in most instances. In any event, the suspect should be ordered to put one hand at a time behind his back and should be handcuffed from behind so that once the officer gets the first cuff on, he in effect can hold the suspect in an arm lock. It is then relatively easy to get the second cuff in place.

After the suspect has been completely handcuffed, the officer should return to a more thorough search. If the officer is going to go through the suspect's wallet, this should be done in full view of the suspect so as to minimize the possibility that he will later claim that some illegal evidence was planted there by the officer.

Recommended Reading

A. F. Brandstatter and Allen A. Hyman, *Fundamentals of Law Enforcement* (Beverly Hills, Calif.: Glencoe Press, 1971), chapter 12, "Patrol Action Involving Other Vehicles."

CHAPTER 9

Specific Tactics and Teamwork

A police officer responding to a call has the difficult job of being mentally prepared to deal with the assignment before he has any real idea of the nature of the call. Based on information given him when he receives his assignment, he must determine whether it is an emergency, whether there is a need for assistance, and whether his arrival is expected or whether the situation warrants secrecy or surprise.

Other factors may also need to be evaluated—the type of area (commercial, residential), the kind of streets (through streets or a dead-end street), and whether any other units are responding to the call. Above all, the officer should keep an open mind and constantly be aware of the element of uncertainty involved in all calls. An officer's barging into a situation, basing his approach entirely on information he received over the police radio, can result and has resulted in disasters. Overreaction by the officer can trigger a similar overreaction on the part of citizens at the scene and may lead to injury or death to some participant.

Some departments have a policy that the radio dispatcher who assigns the call to the beat officer also gives the officer the name and address of the person who reported the incident to the police. Although this system is not foolproof, it can sometimes be of assistance to the officer in evaluating the validity of the complaint. Complaints that come from an address other than the scene of the alleged offense usually indicate at the very least that the caller has only hazy facts concerning the circumstances. Similarly, complaints in which the caller refuses to identify himself or herself or hangs up immediately after giving the information should alert the officer both to the range of possible problems and to the possibility that the call is a hoax.

Over the past few years police officers have been victims of several planned, ambush-type attacks. In some cases the officers were lured to the location of the attack by a telephoned complaint of a disturbance. In other incidents the false report of a disturbance or of a crime allegedly in progress was employed to involve police units at one location while an actual crime was taking place at another.

Assaults and Homicides

An officer responding to an assault or homicide report has several questions with which he must deal almost immediately. The officer's primary responsibility is the protection of life; therefore, once he ascertains what has actually taken place, his first responsibility is to determine the physical condition of the victim. If the victim is injured seriously enough to require hospitalization, the officer should make the necessary transportation arrangements before attempting to investigate the facts surrounding the incident. In many cases the officer will also be called on for some degree of first-aid treatment to the victim.

In cases where the officer is told by someone that the victim is dead, he is still responsible for making his own determination as to whether the victim is in fact deceased. If there is any possibility that the victim is still alive, the officer should arrange for immediate medical assistance or have the victim transported to the hospital.

While a police officer is not empowered to pronounce a person dead, he should be able to use his first-aid training and his field experience to determine when a person "appears" dead. Once he has made this determination, he should immediately undertake the preliminary investigation.

The first and most important step in the preliminary investigation at the scene of a homicide is the protection of the crime scene. Naturally, the crime scene can vary greatly. In a home it may consist of anything from the room where the victim was found to the entire house. Outdoors, it may range from the immediate area where the body was located to an entire field in a rural area.

In practice, most officers conducting a preliminary investigation of a homicide are limited in the size of the area they can actually control and protect. If the officer is working alone and must deal with a homicide in a large building, he should try at the very least to prevent anyone from entering the room in which the body is located. Under no circumstances should he allow any unauthorized persons to disturb the body in any way. In some instances friends or relatives will claim that they must remove some personal belongings from the deceased, such as keys, identification, money, jewelry. The officer in charge of the scene must not allow this.

It may even become necessary for the officer to use force in protecting a homicide scene. While it is understandable that relatives or close friends may feel an obligation to recover some belonging or personal effects, the officer should remember that once a crime scene has been disturbed, no matter how slightly, it can never be returned to its original state.

In the case of a criminal investigation, the need to protect the investigative process takes precedence over the needs or desires of the individual. In normal practice, the only person authorized to remove anything from the body of a deceased is the coroner, and the officer should be present at that time and receive a receipt from the coroner listing all the articles removed. Until the officer in charge of the crime scene either receives a receipt from the coroner or is relieved from this responsibility by his superior, *he* is responsible for the body and all the personal possessions of the victim.

Another important part of preserving the crime scene includes obtaining the identities of all persons who were there when the officer arrived. Particularly because statistics indicate that in the majority of homicide cases the victim and the attacker were known to each other, every attempt should be made to identify all persons present. In crimes of this type the possibility is very good that someone present will have valuable information that can lead to the solution of the case.

Family Disputes

When an officer knows in advance that he is responding to a call involving a family dispute, he should endeavor to make his approach to the matter as low-key as possible. Unless the radio assignment indicated that weapons were involved, a family dispute should not be considered as an emergency assignment calling for the officer to use emergency tactics.

Even though most family disputes involve parties who do not actually want to harm the individual toward whom they are directing their antagonism, the potential for violence in these situations should not be minimized. Former Attorney General Ramsey Clark has pointed out that in the eight-year period starting with 1960, ". . . 93 out of 475 police officers killed in the line of duty died from wounds received answering disturbance calls."[1]

One approach that many officers have found useful in handling a disturbance call where the participants are shouting at each other is to speak in a calm, soft voice. By making no effort to drown out the voices of the antagonists, and in fact making it impossible for his voice to be heard over the shouting, the officer forces the disputing parties to quiet down in order to hear what he has to say. Obviously this tactic will not work in all situations. In many cases the participants *do* want police intervention so that they can back down without losing face. They often are more willing to quiet down and give the officer the opportunity to help them out of their situation. After the officer has restored a degree of quiet, he can take steps to deal with some of the underlying problems that brought about the confrontation.

The key to accomplishing these tasks is to separate the persons involved. Because of close family ties in many such disputes, the individuals involved tend to overreact and to threaten violence that they do not actually intend. By separating them, the officer has afforded them the opportunity to withdraw from their threatening posture without giving the impression that they have backed down. In a sense they have been given the opportunity to back down gracefully from a position they might otherwise have felt obligated to maintain.

Another family problem is a husband-wife fight in which one party attempts to use the officer as a witness to a civil action that he or she intends to institute against the other. For example, the wife might try to provoke the husband into some aggressive action or into making a threat or an admission that she feels the officer would be able to substantiate at a divorce hearing. In this circumstance the officer must make it perfectly clear to both parties that he has no authority to mediate civil problems and that he will be unavailable as a witness to such court action. (Civil cases will be discussed later in the chapter.) If it is clear that the problem is entirely civil, not criminal, the officer should immediately leave. If, however, there has been or is the potential for violence, the officer is obligated to mediate the problem.

In some cases the woman will physically attack her husband in the officer's presence, assuming that it is the officer's duty to protect her from any retaliation. Such cases require deft and prompt handling by the officer. In all family disputes, the officer should refrain from putting his hands on either party unless absolutely necessary. If either party should arm himself with a weapon, such as a knife, or a gun, or, as happens in some instances, a pot of boiling water, the officer must take prompt action to disarm and restrain that person. The officer should not assume that merely because the confrontation is of a family type it is less deserving of his attention or that there is less possibility of someone's being hurt. As Ramsey Clark pointed out, a surprisingly large percentage of officers who have been killed in the line of duty were killed in connection with family disputes.

Despite this statistic, the officer should remember that in most such cases the antagonism is mostly vocal, and if it is handled properly, the potential for violence can be quickly reduced. Any premature use of force by the officer may provoke either or both of the parties to turn on the officer rather than each other.

If one party attacks the other in the officer's presence, the officer should, rather than becoming involved in a protracted wrestling match, decide whether an arrest is justified or necessary and then act accordingly. Obviously, he cannot allow a husband to assault his wife while waiting for her to state that she wants her husband arrested.

Once the officer has decided that action on his part is warranted in order to protect one of the parties from physical harm, he should act quickly and decisively. Obviously, when two officers are at the scene it is much easier to handle the situation than if one officer is working alone. Even if the officer is alone, however, decisive action can turn the situation to his favor. Once he has physically placed the offending party under arrest, the officer should stress to that person that he or she is under arrest and that he or she is required by law to submit to the arrest and the officer's custody. In most such cases it is relatively easy for the officer to impress on the arrested person that he is actually being arrested by his spouse and that the officer is merely carrying out his duty in taking the person into custody.

At this point the arrested spouse sometimes insists that he also wants the other spouse arrested. Since the individual is already in custody, such an arrest is not warranted. However, the officer should explain to the arrested person that he has the right to file a report against the other party and that it will be up to the prosecuting attorney to decide whether a complaint should be issued.

Protracted discussions, arguments, or explanations by the officer once an arrest has been made tend to diminish his authority in the eyes of those involved in the disturbance. Once the suspect has been arrested, explanations by the officer are often viewed as indecision on his part. As soon as practical after the arrest the officer should remove his prisoner from the scene.

An officer should not let himself become involved in a dispute in which one party threatens to have the other arrested if the person does not make some kind of promise regarding his future conduct. In some such instances a wife will threaten to have her husband arrested "unless he promises to quit drinking," or "unless he promises to stop beating me," or "unless he promises to turn his paycheck over to me so that he won't spend it all on liquor." In any such case, the officer is justified in refusing to take the suspect into custody, and referring the complainant to the prosecuting attorney. In addition, the officer should advise the complaining witness that he will file a report of the matter, including the complainant's threat of arrest if the suspect did not comply with his or her wishes. It is partly for the officer's own protection that he should file a report in such cases. When individuals have been unsuccessful in taking advantage of the police officer or his authority, they are sometimes prone to complain later that he failed to perform his duty.

Lastly, and possibly most important, when dealing with family disputes the officer should be alert to the potential for violence and harm to himself. Unlike persons who perpetrate crimes for profit or premeditated crimes, persons who are emotionally involved with each other are unpredictable in their actions. The number of police deaths related to family disputes should serve as ample evidence that the police officer can ill afford to relax his vigilance simply because the parties involved do not come under the general definition of "criminals." Furthermore, it is probable that a great number of the officers killed or injured while intervening in family disputes were killed or injured because they did relax their vigilance, believing that the situation was not potentially dangerous.

Prowler Calls

Another instance in which the patrol officer has little advance knowledge of the type of situation he will encounter is when he responds to a report of a prowler. Often such a report is based merely on the caller's suspicions, aroused by an unusual noise, a shadow, his own fear of being home alone, or even his having seen an upsetting TV show or motion picture. On the other hand, such a report may well indicate an attempt by someone to commit a crime, and for this reason the officer responding should make every effort to ascertain whether a prowler actually has been in the area.

The mere fact that the suspect is identified as a prowler rather than a burglar, a robber, or some other explicit category of offender usually indicates that the caller does not himself know whether a crime is actually involved. Since the term "prowler" does not identify a specific illegal act, the officer responding to the assignment must take care not to be provoked into an overreaction.

While the suspected prowler may be a burglar or a person attempting some other crime, it is also entirely possible that he is a drunk attempting to find a place to "sleep it off," a suspicious suitor trying to check up on his girlfriend, or a juvenile bent more on mischief than on crime. There have been instances when the suspected prowler was an elderly person mistakenly attempting to enter the wrong home. In one such case the owner of the home killed the man, thinking he was a burglar. In another case the prowler report was made by a neighbor, and when the police went unannounced to the designated home, the owner, who knew nothing of the prowler report, killed the officer who was checking his rear door.

If at all possible, an officer should not investigate a prowler call without assistance. An officer alone in the dark can himself be mistaken for a prowler. Two officers working together can check out this kind of call much more quickly and with less risk. While it is sometimes preferable for the officers to arrive at the scene as quietly as possible, once they begin to check the area they should make generous use of their flashlights. The flashlight tends to identify the person using it as someone conducting a search rather than someone attempting to hide. In addition, its use will often flush the person who is the subject of the search out of hiding. Except when the person is attempting to hide after attempting a serious crime, it is a quirk of human nature that many persons will come out voluntarily rather than be discovered hiding. Many times in such situations the suspect chooses to "bluff it out" by attempting to explain his presence or his actions. A common explanation by a prowler discovered on someone else's property is that he needed to urinate and was attempting to do so out of view of the street.

The officer's primary job in responding to a prowler call is to try to ascertain whether there actually was a prowler and if so what his purpose was and to locate and identify him. If the officer can do all these things without injury to anyone, he can justifiably feel that he has successfully completed a potentially dangerous task.

Sexual Offenses

The officer responding to a report of a sexual offense should be prepared to exhibit more tact, diplomacy, and discretion than is usually required in any other type of offense. It is understandable that in cases in which little children are the victims, the parents are likely to be very upset and at the same time very protective of their child. Under such circumstances it is exceedingly difficult for the officer to obtain accurate information. In the case of a girl who has reportedly been raped, for example, if the mother is unwilling to permit the officer to conduct a detailed interview with the child, and there is a male parent or relative present, useful details can sometimes be obtained by interviewing the child out of the presence of the mother. Unless the mother indicates a willingness to discuss the offense in detail, she should not be pressed about the intimate facts of what occurred. In many such cases a physical examination will be performed by a doctor, who is usually successful in obtaining the necessary facts from the child.

It is usually better if the officer does not make specific inquiries of the victim about whether she was raped or was the victim of an unnatural sexual assault. Rather than implanting ideas in the victim's mind, and possibly prejudicing her description of the offense, it is better to encourage the victim to describe the events in her own words.

In cases involving reported sexual assaults against small children, it is understandable that the parents would want to protect the child from having to relive the incident by reciting the details to the police officer. Once the officer is satisfied that the parents are adamant in this position, he should ask whether the child recited the details of the offense to either parent. If one of the parents indicates that he or she does know the full details, the officer can make use of the parent's account of the details as told by the child. The officer should, however, continually ask questions to insure that the reporting parent is repeating what was told by the child and is not expanding on the facts or giving his or her own interpretation of the facts.

If the reported crime is exhibitionism, the officer should take care to ascertain exactly what the victim observed as opposed to what he or she assumed from the suspect's actions. In some incidents of this type, adult women have originally claimed that the suspect lewdly exposed his genitals to them. Under close questioning, police have learned that because of the suspect's actions or attitude they assumed he was exposing himself, but that they had not actually seen him do anything that was obscene and/or illegal. A criminal complaint of this type can be based only on what the victim saw or heard, not what he or she assumed or interpreted something to mean.

In order to ascertain firmly just what the victim or witness actually saw, it is necessary for the investigating officer to ask specific questions and to receive specific answers, for example:

Q.: Where was the suspect when you first observed him?

A.: He was sitting in his car.

Q.: Where were you in relation to the car?

A.: The car was parked at the curb and I was walking by.

Q.: Was the car facing the same direction you were walking?

A.: Yes.

Q.: Was the suspect sitting in the front or back seat? Was he sitting on the side near the curb or away from the curb?

A.: He was sitting behind the wheel away from the curb.

Q.: What did you see?

A.: Well, as I walked by I noticed him motion to me and then motion toward his pants.

Q.: Then what did you do and what did you see?

A.: I kept walking and I noticed him rubbing the front of his pants, so I knew he was playing with himself.

Q.: Did you see anything else?

A.: No, I didn't need to see anything else. I knew what he was doing.

Q.: Did you see him expose his privates at any time?

A.: No, but he probably would have if I had stopped when he motioned to me.

It is obvious that in this situation the victim did not actually see any act that was illegal. She assumed—and probably correctly—that the suspect was attempting to call her attention to his actions, and it was also probably true that his intent and his actions were sexual in nature. However, based on the victim's statements, the only overt actions the suspect took were to motion to the victim and to move his hand in a rubbing motion on the front of his pants. Since the victim stated that she made these observations while walking by the parked car in which the suspect was seated, she had a very brief period in which to make any observations of his actions.

Assuming that the victim can furnish the officer with sufficient evidence with which to identify and locate the suspect—physical description and license number and description of the auto—the officer can investigate the report to the extent of identifying the suspect and checking to see whether any similar reports involving him are on file or whether he has a criminal record, particularly a record for similar offenses.

In instances of reported rape of a teen-age girl, it is important that the officer does not accept the uncorroborated details from the parents. In many such cases the girl is likely to be less truthful or frank with her parents in discussing the details than she will be with a police officer. Here again, the parents may object to having the officer interview their daughter, claiming that it is unnecessary or unwise to make her recall the shocking details. Often in such circumstances the officer can postpone his interview until a later time. He may be able to contact the girl at school or have her come to police headquarters on the pretext of having her look at pictures of suspects. If the identity of the suspect is known to the girl, the officer can explain that it will be necessary for her to discuss the case in detail with the prosecutor before a formal complaint can be issued.

Merely because a teen-age girl is the alleged victim of rape, and the officer feels that she is not likely to be entirely truthful in front of her parents, it should not be assumed that her report is false. It is far more likely that the young woman's reluctance is based on her unwillingness to embarrass either herself or her parents with an account of the details of the offense, sometimes combined with an unwillingness to display to her parents her sexual knowledge.

An alert officer can usually sense this type of situation and can often gain future cooperation from the victim by not pressing her for details in the presence of her parents. Sometimes, while the actual criminal attack was accurately described by the victim, she is reluctant to give details of her activities that might have preceded the attack, feeling that they might make her appear less innocent. Women who met a stranger in a bar or nightclub and were later attacked are understandably reluctant to reveal the circumstances under which they met the suspect.

Unfortunately, some of the stereotyped attitudes that males have held toward females over the years, particularly as they apply to unescorted females who get in trouble while out at night, give some justification to the reluctance of women to relate truthfully all the facts regarding a criminal assault. Whatever the circumstances of the attack, however, a skillful officer who uses tact and diplomacy in his questioning can usually get the necessary facts from the victim. The facts may indicate that some degree of mutual consent was involved or that while the victim may not have consented to the act, she did not forcefully object. Such cases sometimes end up with the criminal charge being something less than forcible rape. Typically, a lesser charge might be simple assault, or, depending on the age of the victim, statutory rape.

Adult women are less reluctant to discuss such offenses in detail, particularly when they are being interviewed privately by only one officer. They usually exhibit more reluctance in front of more than one officer or in the presence of some other third party. Some of the large police departments now have women officers to whom such reports can be made. In most small and medium-sized departments, however, it is up to the regular beat officer, usually male, to take the original report and conduct the preliminary investigation.

A married woman may show an unwillingness to discuss the details of a sexual offense in the presence of her husband. An observant officer can usually quickly spot this reluctance and will not press the point at that time. Above all, an officer taking a report or conducting a preliminary investigation should not do anything to give the impression that he is doubting or questioning the victim's version of the offense. Even if the officer does suspect that the story is either partly or wholly false, he can, by giving the impression that he fully accepts the victim's version, increase the probability that the victim will give information that can be checked for validity.

Civil Cases

The police officer has no authority to adjudicate civil disputes, and once he determines that the call to which he has responded is totally civil, he should notify both parties that he is not empowered to take any action. As a matter of public relations, however, the officer should attempt to refer the parties to an agency that is equipped to deal with their problem.

Once the officer has explained that because the problem is civil he is not authorized to take any action, one or both of the parties may attempt to restate the problem, or to embellish it to make it appear that the other side has committed a criminal offense. The officer should not allow himself to be drawn into the dispute by this tactic, and once he has explained his lack of authority, he should withdraw as soon as possible rather than remaining and becoming a referee between the two parties. The longer he remains at the scene, the more opportunity the participants have to attempt to draw him into the dispute.

A typical case in which the officer may become involved is a husband-wife dispute. This kind of situation has a multitude of variations, ranging from the wife's wanting her husband put out of the house to allegations that one party "stole" money from the other. In almost all cases of this type, the officer's presence is more likely to add fuel to the dispute than to end it. He obviously cannot solve the couple's problems, and his continued presence may well lead one of the parties to attempt to provoke the other into some action that would require the officer's intervention.

A variation of the husband-wife dispute is the couple's fighting over a minor child. Often the couple is separated or divorced, and they have already been advised by a court as to what rights each has. In any event, once the officer determines that some legal ruling has been made, he need only refer the parties to their attorneys if they feel that court orders have been violated. A more complex problem is a couple's disagreement over one or the other's treatment of their children. Again, unless there is a criminal offense involved, the officer should make his position known to both parties and withdraw.

In some instances one of the parties will know that the officer has no jurisdiction because the matter is civil and will order the officer from the home. The officer should not let this attack draw him into the dispute, but again, after making sure that the other party understands his position, he should withdraw.

If the police officer needs any additional reasons for not becoming involved in civil matters, he need only reflect on the amount of time he could spend in court as a witness in civil cases. Such court appearances are rarely reimbursed by his department because the officer's involvement is not viewed as being in the line of duty.

Methods of Approaching Suspected Crime Locations

When the police have received a report of a possible crime in progress, nothing is more discouraging or more indicative of poor planning and organization than to have the police units covering the assignment all approach the scene from the same direction while the suspect or suspects flee in the other. While keeping in mind the necessity for holding radio transmissions to a minimum, all units responding to the assignment should try to make the other units aware of their locations and intended routes to the crime scene. In this way both the units responding and other units in the area will be aware of what routes would be unprotected and available as escape routes. Units not assigned to cover the crime scene will then be able to position themselves in the general area so they can observe any suspicious individuals or cars leaving the area.

Departments usually have set rules or policies covering the use of sirens and red lights when approaching the location of a suspected crime in progress. Generally, the use of the siren and red light is intended as a means of affording the officer the opportunity to reach the scene in as short a time as possible. In most cases, however, it is advisable to turn off the lights and siren before reaching the immediate vicinity of the suspected offense and to make the final approach at a sufficiently slow speed to allow the officer to evaluate the situation. An officer who takes the time to size up the situation before going into action is much more capable of deciding intelligently what action he should take. Additionally, and of equal importance, he is much more capable of protecting his own life.

As an example, a standard rule in some departments is that in response to a report of a crime in progress, police cars will use both red lights and sirens to a point a few blocks from the location of the reported incident. At this point the siren will be cut off to afford as little warning as possible to the suspects if they are still at the scene. If particular care is needed, the radio cars will be told not to use either their sirens or their red lights.

In the case of an armed robbery in progress, it may be that a second suspect is nearby in an auto, acting both as a lookout and as a means of escape. An officer who takes the time to look over the area upon his approach would likely notice a parked car with a person sitting behind the wheel. If he proceeded directly to the crime scene, in all probability he would be able to give a description of the suspect auto. In some cases the first officer arriving at the scene will describe his approach over his radio and at the same time describe any possibly suspicious persons or autos. This enables subsequent officers arriving at the scene to focus their attention on these suspects. Obviously, an officer who arrives at the scene at a normal rate of speed and without using his siren has reduced the probability that the suspects will have advance warning of his approach.

Another point relative to multiple units approaching a crime scene while using their sirens is the possibility of collisions between these units. An officer traveling at high speed with his siren on is unlikely to hear the approach of another police unit traveling under similar conditions. However, if each officer is aware that other units are responding and also knows the general route or direction from which they are approaching, he will be alert for them and much less likely to become involved in an accident.

There is something about a high-speed chase or a response to a radio assignment that tends to cause many officers to lose their objectivity and take unnecessary risks. A few years ago I observed just such a situation in which ten police units were involved in a high-speed chase of an auto that had fled the scene of a warehouse burglary. The police radio dispatcher was receiving constant information regarding the position and direction of the suspect auto and was positioning the radio units not directly involved in the chase so that they were able to effectively cut off all escape routes. Despite this, three of the police cars became involved in collisions with each other, thereby eliminating these units from the chase. One of these units was so severely damaged that it could not be moved immediately and it blocked off the pursuit of several other units. Unorganized chases such as this are not only wasteful of police manpower and expertise, but they constitute a high-risk operation, endangering both lives and property.

On some types of assignments, the officer approaching the location of a reported crime will find it to his advantage to pull to the curb and to stop once he gets within view of the suspected location. Particularly in instances where the information he received from the radio dispatcher is vague or nonspecific as to what type of illegal activity is suspected, the officer may want to size up the situation before moving in. Suspicious activity, such as a large gathering of people or an unusually large number of cars parked in the area, may be a clue as to what type of problem is to be expected. In a case where the officer observes a crowd, his judgment regarding his action or approach may well be shaped by the average age of the group. Seemingly small matters, such as age, type of dress, type of neighborhood, time of day, and even the day of the week, can often be indicators of the type of disturbance or gathering that the officer may encounter.

A large gathering of teen-agers in the vicinity of a school may indicate a fight in progress. A group of two or three people, especially at night, may overreact when they spot the police car, trying to give the impression that they are all friends just "clowning around," or one or two members of the group may attempt to walk off casually. Such a situation may be an indication that one of the members of the group has been the victim of a "drunk rolling" or a strong-arm robbery.

A group of a dozen or more adults often indicates some type of disagreement in progress. If the members of the group are well dressed, however, it is unlikely that the disagreement will result in violence. It seems to be a natural human reaction that people who are well dressed go out of their way to avoid any physical contact that might damage their clothes. There have been instances when an officer has been dispatched to investigate a large adult gathering. If it is Sunday, and if the people are near a church, the gathering is usually a social one at the termination of the services. Some persons phone police headquarters to report such gatherings (usually anonymously) simply because they resent the presence of these groups.

Obviously, good judgment dictates that an officer should not become involved in some situations alone. In responding to a robbery in progress, a riot, or a fight involving weapons, a single officer is at a marked disadvantage. Experience and good judgment may dictate that an officer delay his final approach to the scene until assured that he has cover. Despite this, and possibly because he believes that he needs to prove his fearlessness, an officer will sometimes go it alone in situations that can well result in his injury or death or in his being captured and held hostage.

A method sometimes used in approaching a crime scene or area of suspected disturbance at night is for the officer to turn off both his lights and his engine approximately a block away from the destination. By coasting along, the officer is less likely to alert any persons involved in criminal actions and is more likely to hear any unusual sounds such as loud voices, screams, or calls for help.

As mentioned earlier, detailed familiarity with the neighborhood is of invaluable assistance to an officer responding to an assignment, and the more he knows about the location before his arrival, the better equipped he is to deal with the situation. For example, if the officer recognizes the address to which he is assigned as being a business place that is ordinarily closed at that hour, he can deduce that there was possibly an illegal entry and that he will need assistance in covering all possible points of exit. He may also logically assume that if a burglary is in progress, the suspect or suspects might have a vehicle in the area.

In several instances of burglary, officers have been able to locate the point of entry but unable to find a suspect. After finding a suspicious auto parked in the area, the officers have withdrawn, leaving one or two of their number to stake out the car. On several occasions this method has proved successful, and the officers have apprehended the suspect returning to his car with evidence in his possession sufficient to connect him with the burglary.

Similarly, in instances where only one or two officers are available to search a large building, patience is often their best tool. In some cases the risk of bodily harm to the officers makes a detailed search of the premises inadvisable. In such situations an officer can sometimes conceal himself in the building so that he has a vantage point from which to view the most likely areas where a person might be concealed. It is typical of persons who are hiding from the police to feel compelled to leave the premises as soon as they feel that the search for them has been discontinued. An officer's patience in waiting out such a situation will sometimes be rewarded by capture of the suspect.

If the officer has remained concealed for what he feels is a reasonable length of time and has had no results, he can employ a final ruse. The officer leaves the building, trying to give the impression that the search is being discontinued—turning out all lights, ascertaining that doors and windows are locked, and so on. If he has a partner, the partner can remain inside. If the officer is working alone, he can stake out the place by moving off some distance in his patrol car but still situating himself so that he keep the most logical escape route under observation.

Teamwork among Officers

An all-important ingredient to the successful coverage of patrol assignments is teamwork between officers. Understanding between partners is an absolute must—understanding about both their method of handling assignments and the manner in which they protect each other. Experienced officers who have worked together for an extended period of time exhibit a degree of efficiency and unspoken cooperation that immediately labels them as highly competent professionals.

An example of putting knowledge and cooperation to their full use is commonly seen when a two-man unit of experienced officers responds to a report of a burglary in progress. As the unit heads for the location, the officers pool their knowledge of the area or address—type of building, residential or commercial area, type of alarm (if any), number and location of exits, whether the building should be lighted. On arrival the only words spoken between them may be one officer saying, "I'll take the front." The other officer will move quickly to the rear of the building, taking care to keep his gear—keys, whistle, and handcuffs—from jangling. The second officer will take his cue regarding the method of approach and search from the tactics he expects his partner to use. If he expects the officer at the front of the building to make a show of trying the door and flashing his light inside, he knows that this is a ruse intended to provoke the suspect or suspects into attempting to flee out the rear toward him.

Teamwork extends to all facets of police work and is equally important in day-to-day contacts with citizens. No matter how trivial an assignment may seem, the officers should not become careless to the extent that they forget the potential for danger that is a part of their profession. Any time a team of officers is questioning an individual, one of them should take the lead in the conversation or interrogation, while the second officer listens and looks and at the same time stations himself in a position that affords the greatest assistance to his partner. Two officers should avoid standing side by side while interrogating a suspect. Neither should one be directly in front of the suspect while the second officer is directly behind the man. Each officer can afford his partner better cover if they are at right angles to each other—that is, if one officer is directly in front of the suspect and his partner is on one side of the person and slightly out of arm's reach. Similarly, on approaching a suspect or a crime scene, two officers should take care that they are not side by side. By spreading out, they not only present a smaller and more difficult target, but they are viewing the situation from different angles that might afford one of them a quicker warning of danger.

When two or more officers are conducting a search with flashlights, each officer should know where the other officers are and take care not to outline another officer in the beam of his light. Aside from identifying the officer's location for anyone hiding nearby, the light effectively blinds the other officer so that he would be at a disadvantage if he had to defend himself at that moment. When using a flashlight during a search, the officer should take care that he is not holding his light directly in front of his body. If a suspect is desperate enough to attempt to shoot his way out, a natural tendency is to shoot directly at the beam of light. An experienced officer will always hold his light as far to the side as possible.

If the assignment involves the search of a building, an effective search must be methodical and coordinated. An uncoordinated search leads to escape routes being left unprotected, some areas being searched several times, and other locations being over-looked entirely. If each team or group of officers has a specific area of responsibility, the result will be a systematic and thorough search that can be completed in much less time than if the problem were handled haphazardly.

Experienced officers who have worked as a team for a period of time develop such cooperation that they are able to function as a unit without having to talk over each situation in advance. In some situations one officer may develop better rapport with certain individuals than his partner. Some persons are particularly adept in talking with children, for example, or older people. The same person may be weak in conversing with persons of certain races or in talking to women.

When each partner knows and recognizes both his and his partner's strengths and limitations in these areas it is much easier for them to function in a way that allows them to take full advantage of their own strengths and weaknesses. This does not mean, however, that when one officer takes over an interview or an interrogation his partner should stand passively by and not be involved. Often the person watching and listening to a conversation rather than taking part in it is better able to spot weaknesses or faults in the statements being made by the person being questioned. Additionally, the partner who does not have to direct all his attention to the interview has the opportunity to observe what impact the conversation with the citizen is having on the people around them. If other persons close by are listening to the conversation, they often give indications that the person interviewed is not telling the truth. Bystanders to such conversations, particularly if they are not aware of being closely observed, will often flinch, frown, smile, or become startled if they hear the person lying or misstating the truth.

The officer who notices these clues while his partner is conducting most of the conversation may merely want to store this information for a later follow-up rather than challenging the witness at that time. If the person undergoing an interview and the bystander are friends, they are likely to help each other in "cleaning up" or reinforcing their story once they become aware that the officers have some suspicion that the information being given is not entirely accurate.

An officer can make a multitude of other observations that will be helpful to an investigation while his partner is conducting an interview—a bystander who is too casual in leaving the scene, a potential piece of evidence that someone picks up or attempts to conceal, or a bystander who is too concerned with attempting to overhear the conversation between the officer and the person being interviewed. Police officers do not operate in a vacuum. Their mere presence often provokes actions, reactions or interactions that would not otherwise have taken place. It is especially true that when an individual is guilty of some criminal act or has guilty knowledge, his sense of guilt is very likely to be heightened by the presence of the officers. He is prone to give some indication of his guilt, no matter how slight. It is the job of a good officer to be able to spot this signal and interpret it.

CHAPTER 10

Crime
Scene
Investigations

The basic purposes of a crime scene investigation are the preservation, recovery, identification, and evaluation of potential information.

Necessity for Detailed Observations

While it is understandable that a great deal of emphasis is placed on the search for evidence, the determination of what constitutes evidence in a particular investigation can be made only when all the available information has been recovered and evaluated. It follows, therefore, that one of the first and most important functions of the first officer arriving at the scene of a crime is to make careful and detailed observations. It should be presumed that before any examination or investigation of a crime scene is begun by the investigators, the scene is exactly as it was left by the perpetrator of the offense. Merely walking into a room where a crime was committed can contaminate potential evidence. For example, any foreign material found on the floor of the room is much more credible evidence if it was observed and recovered before anyone had an opportunity to walk through the room.

For an officer initiating a preliminary investigation at a crime scene, important observations should include the time of day and the lighting conditions that existed when he first observed the scene. The seemingly minor point of lighting can be important because in certain situations the fact that no lights were on in a home or business place when the officer arrived might indicate whether or not the crime was committed during daylight hours. On the other hand, if the officer switched on the lights as he entered the room and immediately began his examination, he might forget that the room was unlighted when he initially entered.

Often a slow, systematic observation by the officer, using a clockwise examination of the area in which the crime took place, can be used to insure that the area is thoroughly covered. In addition, such a visual examination can be used to divide the area later into quadrants so that the officer can complete his examination, and later his search for information, in a more systematic manner.

Generally, after the officer has made a detailed observation of the crime scene, he is better able to determine how large or small an area it will be necessary for him to keep under protective control to prevent intrusion by unauthorized persons. While it is standard procedure in some larger departments for the patrol officer who first arrives at a crime scene merely to protect and preserve the scene pending the arrival of investigators, in most smaller departments the patrol officer has the added responsibility of instituting his own preliminary investigation.

Recovery and Preservation of Evidence

As mentioned earlier, the determination of what is or is not evidence cannot always be made at the crime scene. In many criminal investigations a great deal of information is gathered and analyzed before even a few legitimate pieces of evidence can be recovered. One example of evidence that has proved pertinent in several investigations was the recovery by an investigating officer of a piece of mud from the carpet in a room where a homicide had taken place. The mud could have been left there by any of several persons who were not involved in the crime. It was also possible that it had come from the shoe of the person responsible for the crime. Since the officer who originally examined the scene observed the mud before he entered the room, the possibility that he had brought the mud into the room was eliminated.

The subsequent investigation disclosed that the people who could have left the mud at the crime scene innocently had no traces of such mud on any of their shoes. The general area surrounding the crime scene was dry, eliminating the possibility that the mud came from there. However, once the investigation focused on a particular suspect, traces of the same type of mud were found on the brake pedal of his auto.

Whenever the investigating officer discovers some type of evidence that he feels may be pertinent to an investigation, he should first make a written record, describing the article and its location. For example, if an officer investigating a burglary found wood shavings below a window that was suspected of being the burglary point of entry, he should first make a written description of the find. Typically, the written description might state: "Wood shavings, apparently freshly cut, unpainted, found in small pile outside the window to bedroom No. 2. Shavings were closely grouped, in area approx. 10 inches in diameter."

The next step would be for the officer to have the shavings photographed. At least two photographs should be taken from different locations. This makes it easier to describe or possibly explain in court the exact location where the evidence was found. After the potential evidence has been described and photographed, the officer can take steps to recover it for possibly laboratory examination and preservation.

This same technique should apply to the recovery of latent fingerprints. Inasmuch as the possibility always exists that fingerprints can be damaged or destroyed at the time they are dusted or lifted, they should first be photographed if at all possible.

Once the decision is made to preserve potential evidence, great care should be taken to preserve it in the same condition in which it was found. While it is a general practice for the officer recovering evidence to put some personal identification on it, it is often better to seal the evidence in a container and then put the officer's identifying mark on the container. Sometimes when an article must be preserved for later laboratory examination, but when it should be handled as little as possible and not be allowed to come in contact with the material in which it is being preserved, the officer is often forced to rig up some means of suspending the potential piece of evidence by strings or similar material inside a box or other container.

In one case a revolver taken from a suspect was believed to have been used to club the victim to death, and the crime lab was a considerable distance away. The officers suspected that the butt of the weapon might carry traces of blood and human hair from the victim, and it was therefore necessary to protect this part of the weapon from contact with any container that could conceivably remove the potential evidence on contact. The officer who recovered the weapon was able to secure and protect the weapon inside a five-gallon cardboard ice cream container by fastening strings at the hammer, the trigger guard, and the end of the barrel and then running the strings through small holes in the ends of the container and knotting the ends of the strings to each other on the outside. This effectively secured the weapon so that it could be transported with little risk that its butt would come in contact with any material that might remove or damage potential evidence.

While the individual officer may view it as an unnecessary precaution and a waste of time to go to such lengths to protect all the potential evidence he discovers at a crime scene, he should keep in mind that any time evidence he has recovered is introduced in court, it must conform to very stringent rules relative to its admissibility. The officer must be prepared to state under oath the time and location at which the evidence was found, and he must be able to identify the evidence positively as the actual article he recovered. It is common for a defense attorney to ask the officer to describe both how he knows that the evidence in court is the exact same article he recovered, and also what steps he took to protect and preserve it. Questions of this type involve the chain of possession during the entire time the evidence was with the police or the prosecutors.

While the officer who originally recovered the evidence has little or no control over it once he submits it for further examination, he personally must be able to account for the location and method of storage of the evidence until he formally submitted it for examination or safekeeping.

Labeling and Identifying Evidence

No matter how thorough and effective a job the officer does in examining the crime scene and recovering potential evidence, his efforts can be useless unless he is able to identify the evidence presented in court as the same article he recovered at the crime scene. It is because physical evidence cannot lie and cannot be impeached that it carries such weight in a criminal trial.

As a general rule, potential evidence includes any item that indicates that a crime was committed or anything that might connect a particular person to the scene of the crime. This includes, but is not limited to, fingerprints, footprints, hair, blood, tools, or articles of clothing. Some unusual articles that have been recovered at crime scenes and that later proved valuable in investigations include a comb from which strands of hair were recovered for use in identifying the suspect, a bloodstained shirt recovered from the suspect's home and which he had claimed became stained when he rubbed up against a steer carcass in a frozen food locker (analysis of the stains later proved them to be human blood), and a telephone message left for the suspect at a hotel desk. The message was important because the suspect had denied knowing the victim, who was found murdered, but the message indicated that she had phoned him approximately an hour before the crime was committed. Almost anything can turn out to be evidence in a case.

As mentioned, items of evidence should be described and/or photographed before they are moved, and they must be marked for identification and stored for transportation and preservation. The officer marks evidence by affixing his own identifying mark

—his initials, his signature, his department serial number, or any individual mark that he regularly uses as his own distinctive and personal identification.

The most common types of evidence that the officer will be called upon to recover, mark for identification, and submit as evidence include such things as guns, knives, clubs, and various types of narcotics. Narcotics, like such items as hair, blood, and clothing fibers, are usually best stored in plastic envelopes that can be sealed shut. While some officers still put an identifying mark on a gun, it is usually sufficient for the officer merely to record the weapon's serial number in his notebook along with the date and location of the recovery. Needless to say, the officer should be careful when affixing his mark not to destroy any potential evidence. There have been instances in which an officer put his identifying mark on a weapon in such a way as to ruin fingerprints or other markings. Although tying an identification card to the weapon with a piece of twine is not the best method of identifying it, it is sometimes preferable to risking destroying evidence.

Fingerprints, as discussed earlier, should be photographed before an attempt is made to lift them whenever possible. The tools that are available for lifting fingerprints tend to assure that, once lifted, the fingerprints are preserved in a semipermanent manner. An officer who either lifted or observed the lifting of a print should put all pertinent information on the back of the card on which the print is mounted. Important and relevant information includes the date and the location of the recovery—the address plus the exact location of recovery, such as bedroom window sill, back of inside rearview mirror on car, inside doorknob of front door, and so on. After this information is furnished the officer marks it.

In some situations the evidence will consist of a photograph taken at the scene. Obviously, unless a Polaroid-type picture is taken, the officer will not have the opportunity to mark the back of the picture for identification at the time the picture is taken. Instead, the officer can place some personal item such as his police badge, shield, or identification card next to the evidence so that it will be photographed at the same time. The officer should then record in his notebook a description of the picture taken, the date and location, and the article that was used in the picture as his identifying mark.

In the case of articles of evidence that cannot easily be marked directly and are stored in plastic envelopes, the officer may enclose a small identification card in the envelope or mark the necessary identifying information on the outside.

Documenting the Chain of Possession

As was pointed out earlier, it is all-important that the prosecution be able to document the chain of possession of any evidence. Simply put, this means that a permanent record must be maintained that will show where the evidence was at all times, under whose responsibility it was being kept, and who had access to it for examination purposes.

An officer who recovered an important piece of evidence at a crime scene may be called upon months later to identify it, testify as to the circumstances surrounding its recovery, and tell exactly where it has been since he originally recovered it. Under such questioning he need only refer to the property record, one copy of which is generally attached to the evidence at all times. If properly kept, this record should account for the location of the evidence at all times between the original recovery and the presentation of the article in court. Any gap in time that cannot be accounted for in written records may well mean that the evidence will not be admitted in court.

An experienced officer will refuse to handle or transport any article of evidence without first signing a receipt for it, and similarly, he will insist on receiving a receipt for it when he originally turns it in for examination after its recovery.

Systematic Examination and Search

A systematic search of a crime scene not only eliminates duplication of effort but insures that no area will be inadvertently skipped by the searchers. While it is more time-consuming, it is sometimes better to have the crime scene searched by only one officer. If the area is too large for a single officer to handle, or if the use of several officers will increase the thoroughness of the search, careful planning should be done beforehand to insure that all areas are covered.

A large crime scene area can often be divided into sections to simplify a systematic search by several officers. In some cases it is even wise actually to divide the area physically by stretching string so that each officer will know the exact area he is responsible for searching. Smaller areas, such as rooms or offices, can usually be divided in half or into quarters to facilitate a systematic search. If the search is being conducted by two officers, it is often advantageous for one officer to work in a clockwise direction, while the second officer conducts his search in a counterclockwise direction. Whichever method is used, the overall aim should be to insure a complete, systematic search.

In searching an enclosed area, such as a room, it is often advisable for the investigating officer or officers to stop first at the entrance to the room and make detailed observations from there. They should visually examine the other walls, the ceiling, light fixtures, windows, furniture, pictures, and curtains. Later it may prove important for the officer to have noticed whether any article of furniture seemed out of place, whether the curtains were drawn, and whether the windows were open, closed and locked, or closed and unlocked.

If no lights were on in the room, the switches should be checked to see whether the lights were in operating order. In some cases officers have turned the lights on and discovered evidence hidden inside the light fixture.

As with so many areas of criminal investigation, the officer should have the ability to improvise and be flexible enough to adapt his methods to each individual situation.

Witnesses—Cooperative and Uncooperative

Witnesses can serve many purposes to an investigator. They can be of assistance in filling in previously unknown facts; they can tend to verify information received from other sources; they can be used to discount unproved theories; and they can be used as a further investigative tool.

In most criminal investigations in which there is more than one person who claims to have witnessed the offense, the accounts given by the witnesses will vary in some detail. This does not indicate, however, that one witness is wrong or that one witness is giving false information. Different people have different concepts of time, size, distance, and almost anything else that is subject to description. Despite these differences, thorough interrogation by the investigating officer can extract accurate information from each potential witness that can be used to reconstruct the details of the offense accurately.

As pointed out earlier, some witnesses tend to be influenced by what other persons claim to have seen or heard, and the officer who instituted any preliminary investigation should identify and separate all potential witnesses at the earliest possible moment. Care should be taken in the questioning of witnesses to insure that each person is relating what he himself has seen or heard, not what he was told or what he heard someone else say. A witness should not be prevented from giving opinions or impressions, as long as these bits of information are clearly identified as such and not stated as facts.

Not all witnesses are cooperative. This does not mean, however, that all uncooperative witnesses are somehow involved in the offense. Reasons that a witness may not want to volunteer information have been mentioned in earlier chapters—he may have personal feelings about the offense or about some of the persons involved in the offense; he may not want to be viewed by some of his acquaintances as an informer; he may not want to become involved with the police or in appearances in court. With uncooperative witnesses it is all the more important for the officer conducting the preliminary investigation to do a thorough job of discovering what details each witness knows. Once the witness has indicated that he has certain information, he can usually be persuaded to cooperate in the further investigation or in a trial.

As mentioned in an earlier chapter, persons who are believed to be witnesses to an offense but who deny having any information should still be thoroughly questioned and pinned down as to what they deny having seen or heard. Particularly if the witness is friendly to a person accused of a crime, he may, after denying to the police that he has any information, later testify for the defense. If this witness had been required to state in writing that he did or did not have first-hand information concerning certain facts, his ability to change his story later would be decreased.

Sketching the Crime Scene

While photographs of a crime scene serve a very useful purpose, both in assisting the investigation and in court testimony, a sketch of the scene has advantages too. Stains, burns, and wet spots, for example, are often difficult to photograph. In a sketch, the officer can note on a diagram where these things were located. He can even give an exact location by measurements, such as stating that a blood spot was on the rug ten feet from the south wall and eight feet from the west wall (see Figure 3). Similarly, in describing any other article relevant to the investigation—a weapon, a piece of furniture, a body, a cigarette—its location can be marked in a sketch and its exact location noted by measurements.

If the accuracy of the measurements may be of importance to further investigations or at a trial, distances should be measured exactly and not estimated. If two officers work together taking measurements, both officers should note the results and be able to verify them.

While it is not necessary for an officer sketching a crime scene to be an artist, he should be thorough. The overall size of the area should be measured, as should the location of movable articles such as furniture. When an officer makes a crime scene sketch, he seldom if ever knows which measurements may be of future importance. For this reason it is far better for him to include superfluous information than to discover too late than an important detail has been omitted.

Recommended Reading

Roy Wilkins and Ramsey Clark, *Search and Destroy* (New York: Metropolitan Applied Research Center, Inc., 1973). Of particular interest in connection with the preceding chapter 3 of the book, which deals with the police raid on the apartment of Fred Hampton. Included in the text are several excellent crime scene diagrams and photographs.

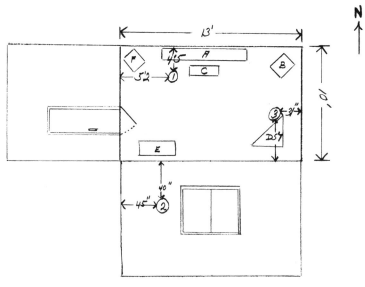

A - Sofa
B - Chair #1
C - Coffee Table
D - Piano
E - Stereo
F - Chair #2

① - BLOOD STAINED KNIFE
② - BLOOD SPOTS ON WALL
③ - BLOOD-STAINED TOWEL

Location: Living Room of apt. #302, 1710 - 14th St., N.W., Washington, D.C.

Arrived at scene 2215 hours, 10 July 1974. Door partly open. Lights off. Window closed and locked. Stereo turned on to radio" with volume turned to maximum, but no station tuned in.

D.P. 5451 P

Figure 3

CHAPTER 11

Traffic
Accident
Investigations

At the scene of a traffic accident, an officer must help injured persons, identify and question witnesses, diagram the scene, and recover evidence.

Dealing with Injured Persons

After a vehicle accident the officer may often encounter injured persons or persons who claim to be injured. In the case of a person who has obviously suffered injury, the officer should undertake whatever first-aid treatment is necessary and make arrangements to have the person transported to a hospital before he undertakes the accident investigation.

In some vehicle accidents one of the parties involved may claim to be injured merely for insurance purposes. In this type of situation, where there is no apparent injury and no need for first-aid treatment, the officer should merely inquire whether the individual wishes to be sent to the hospital. He should not become involved as a witness as to whether the individual is in fact injured.

In his written report of the accident, the officer should describe any apparent injuries and also mention claims of injuries that any of the involved parties make. If an injury is claimed without any visible substantiation, however, the officer should clearly note the fact. In addition, he should note whether or not the injured person agreed to go to a hospital for treatment or examination. One sample report form is shown as Figure 4.

The primary purpose for being so specific and detailed in this part of the accident report is to lessen the probability of the officer's being involved at a later time in a civil suit. In many cases persons institute civil suits for claimed injuries and attempt to use the police officer as a witness to back up their claims of injury. While such claims are often justified, and courtroom testimony in such cases is a necessary part of the officer's job, his practice of detailing injuries and claims of injuries in his report will appreciably decrease the number of times he will be called upon as a witness in cases that were instituted merely because of the possible financial gain.

Witnesses

After caring for any injured parties, the officer's second duty is to obtain the identities of the driver or drivers and all witnesses to the accident. The witnesses will include the passengers in the cars and any persons on the street who claim to have observed the accident.

An important point to remember is that any person involved in the accident, whether he or she admits to witnessing any part of it or not, should be identified in the officer's report. Some vehicle accident cases result in criminal charges against some party. Other accidents later develop into high-priced civil suits. Either type of case may revolve on the word of witnesses. As with a criminal investigation, the officer should attempt to identify potential witnesses and obtain a written statement from these witnesses regarding what they did or did not observe. When the

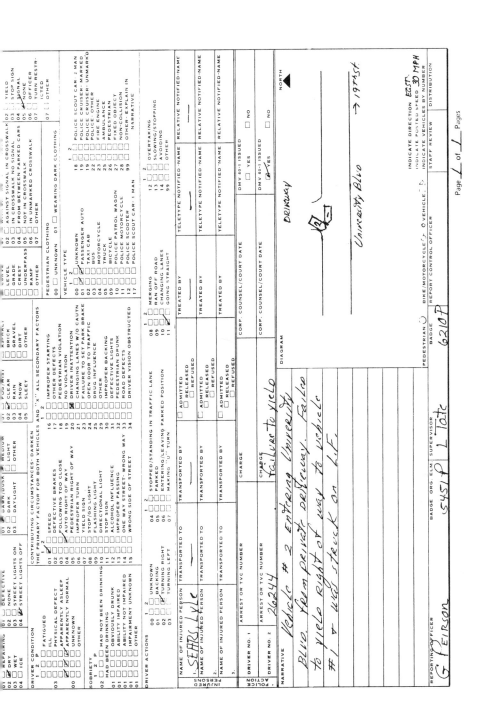

Figure 4

Figure 4 (continued)

officer can show that he made a systematic effort to obtain the identities of all potential witnesses at the scene, it greatly reduces the probability that someone unknown to him will come forward at a later date and claim to have witnessed the incident.

As with the statements taken from witnesses of criminal offenses, the officer taking a statement at an accident should incorporate into the statement facts that clearly indicate the point from which the witness made his or her observations, what was heard in addition to what was seen, and what the witness did not see or hear, particularly as it applies to statements made by other witnesses. Again, as with the statement taken in connection with a criminal offense, any point the witness makes of a negative nature, such as denying that something occurred, or denying that he saw or heard something, should be included.

Diagramming the Accident Scene

After taking care of any injured parties and identifying potential witnesses, the officer's next task is to diagram the accident scene. Because of the importance of this aspect of accident investigation, whenever possible two officers should be assigned to investigate the accident. While one of them is taking care of the injured and obtaining witnesses, the second officer can be protecting the evidence at the scene and verifying such factors as skid marks and point of impact.

Because it is often necessary to remove the vehicles and the debris from the roadway as soon as possible, the officer should first mark the locations of all vehicles or parts of vehicles. In most cases, he first marks the location of all four wheels on the cars involved. This is usually done in chalk, and notations, such as "LF," "LR," "RF," and "RR," should be made to indicate which direction each auto was facing. In addition, each auto should be identified, usually by arbitrarily deciding at the beginning of the investigation to label one auto as "No. 1" and the other as "No. 2." As long as the same identification numbers are assigned throughout the report, a mixup is unlikely.

Skid marks are valuable as evidence in determining such things as speed, direction, and point of impact. Additionally, skid marks often indicate whether the car was under control at the time of the accident and whether all four of its brakes were operating properly. Often, when one of the drivers insists that he stopped at an intersection and then proceeded to cross it before being struck by the other car, his skidmarks will indicate that he skidded completely through the area where he claimed to have stopped, right up to the point of impact. Here again, the officer should use chalk to mark the skid marks for later measurement and diagramming.

In many auto accidents the point of impact becomes all-important in assigning responsibility. Often the final resting points of the vehicles are not a true indication of the point of impact. Usually, the general point of impact can be determined by the location of glass fragments from either of the car's headlights. A more exact point of impact can sometimes be determined by small piles of dirt, which a careful examination of the scene will disclose. When two cars come together in a violent impact, unless they are both new, quantities of dirt will be shaken loose from under the front fenders. Unlike headlight glass, which will be somewhat scattered, such dirt tends to fall in an area of not over a few feet and is generally accepted as a valid indication of the actual point of impact.

A third indicator of the point of impact is sideways skid marks. These are relatively easy to identify and look somewhat like a giant erasure on the pavement. In some cases ordinary skid marks will lead up to the point of impact and suddenly turn at a sharp right angle for several feet. This is usually accepted in court as indisputable evidence of the point of impact. In locating the point exactly, however, allowances must be made for which wheel laid down the skid mark and what part of the auto received the impact. By knowing the exact width and length of the car, the exact point can then be determined within a foot.

Whenever an accident scene is to be diagrammed, all measurements should be made in relation to some fixed point. In some instances the fixed point can be a fire hydrant, a street manhole cover, or a nearby electric light pole. When the accident took place at or near an intersection with marked crosswalks, it is a good practice to use the point at which two of the crosswalk lines intersect at right angles with the curb as a reference.

Recovering or Photographing Evidence

The same rules that apply for handling evidence at a crime scene apply at an accident investigation. The officer conducting the investigation should remember that the accident can possibly become the basis of criminal charges.

Whenever possible, the scene should be photographed in order to back up diagrams of the locations of the cars and potential evidence. Particularly in cases where the mere handling of evidence may destroy it, it should be photographed before being handled. Broken glass that is used as a reference point for the location of the original impact should also be photographed, along with the dirt that may have been left there from the underside of the fenders.

In hit-and-run cases, it is particularly important to retain pieces of shattered glass found at the scene as evidence. Often such glass can be matched with that from a suspected auto. In cases where a suspected hit-and-run car struck a fixed or hard object, it is often possible to collect paint samples for future matching. Using a sharp, clean knife, the investigating officer can usually scrape this paint directly into a clean envelope. In order to prevent possible contamination of the scrapings, the envelope should then be sealed and marked for identification.

Last, in some cases the investigating officer may be able to discern tread markings left by an auto in a hit-and-run case. Again, these markings should be photographed at the earliest possible time before any other method of preserving them is attempted. At the time the photograph is taken, a ruler should be laid across some part of the tread markings in order to give an accurate impression of the width of the tread and the distances between the individual grooves. If the tread markings were left in a soft material, such as tar or dirt, it may be possible to produce a plaster impression of them. If the investigating officer has to request someone else to construct a plaster cast, he can protect the evidence until the arrival of a technician by placing a box or some similar article over it. Whatever article is used to protect the imprint should not be allowed to touch the evidence.

Increasingly, a police investigation of a vehicle accident is used as the primary source from which civil responsibility is determined. Insurance companies routinely base their legal arguments on the findings of the police accident investigator. Many law enforcement officials feel that the police should not be made responsible for investigating and determining responsibility in civil suits. However, in some instances the accident investigation will ultimately be the basis for criminal as well as civil charges. For this reason it is imperative that the investigating officer conduct a thorough investigation. In instances where the case is only civil, it will often not be necessary for the officer to make a judgment as to guilt or responsibility for the accident. He need only conduct a thorough investigation and document in his report all the available evidence, so that determinations as to responsibility can be made by others from the report.

Because most such investigations result in civil rather than criminal charges, it has become a habit among many police accident investigators to do a less than complete or adequate investigation. However, the investigating officer has no way of knowing, at the time of his investigation, whether the case will be a run-of-the-mill, minor civil matter or a serious felony case. One approach that the conscientious officer can take to routine traffic investigations is to view them as a training process, or a method by which he can sharpen his investigative skills. In some instances he can evaluate his completed report against other accident reports to ascertain the quality of his investigation. In this way the officer can gain valuable on-the-job training in actual situations where mistakes due to inexperience or lack of knowledge are not likely to be harmful.

Skill as a traffic accident or vehicle accident investigator is a valuable tool. A patrol officer cannot specialize and only conduct certain types of investigations, he must be knowledgeable in all types, In a very real sense, he must be a generalist rather than a specialist, with skills that can be adapted to any situation.

Recommended Reading

Chapter 17, "Motor Vehicle Homicides," in *Fundamentals of Criminal Investigation*, by Charles E. O'Hara (Springfield, Ill.: Charles C. Thomas, 1967).

CHAPTER 12

Use of
Police
Weapons

The police officer is authorized to use various types of weapons. For the uniformed officer these usually include his service revolver and his baton or night stick. In some instances the officer may be authorized to carry a shotgun, a carbine, and a chemical agent such as mace.

In order to see the use of the service revolver in its proper perspective, and at the same time to understand fully when it should be used, the officer needs to recognize its primary purpose. The gun is intended as a means of killing. This simple statement rules out the use of the gun to threaten someone or to warn him that the officer intends to kill or is capable of killing. Because of news media accounts, many persons—law enforcement personnel and citizens alike—have a misconception regarding the proper use of the weapon by a police officer. It is still not entirely uncommon, after a police officer has shot and killed a suspected criminal, to hear citizens complain that the officer could just as easily have shot to wound the suspect rather than killing him.

One of the worst things that could happen in police law enforcement would be for police officers to be authorized to shoot persons with the intent of wounding them in order to capture or subdue them. In effect, such a ruling would be a license to kill in situations where lethal force was not justified. An officer, after killing a person in a questionable situation, would only need to claim that his intent was to wound the person in order to effect his capture, and that the killing was therefore accidental. As long as it is understood and accepted that the purpose of the weapon is to kill, and that the officer is justified in shooting only when he has reasonable cause to believe that his attempt to kill is justified, the number of situations in which an officer will be justified in shooting is greatly diminished.

These guidelines would also apply to the use of a shotgun and carbine. Each of them is a lethal weapon intended for killing and not for any other purpose. In some respects, the carbine is a more dangerous and lethal weapon than a shotgun. Its striking and penetrating power make it an extremely dangerous weapon to use in many situations. In California a few years ago, officers were conducting a narcotics raid on an apartment. During the raid one of the officers inadvertently fired his carbine while it was pointed at the ceiling. The bullet went through the ceiling and through the floor of the apartment upstairs and struck and killed an innocent person in that apartment.

An officer who fully understands the purpose and potential of his weapon is much better equipped to make intelligent and rational decisions regarding whether he should use his gun than is the officer who has a general belief that his gun can settle arguments, enforce his orders, or merely incapacitate potential attackers.

When to Draw a Weapon

Hard and fast guidelines dictating when an officer is justified in drawing his weapon cannot be effectively made. Such decisions should and must be left with the individual officer, and he must base it on his professional evaluation of the situation and the narrow definition of the purpose of the weapon. If the officer has reasonable cause to believe that his life or the life of some other person is threatened, or that anyone is threatened with great bodily harm, he is duty bound to be prepared to use lethal force to prevent the assault. Obviously, there will be many situations in which the officer will feel it necessary to draw his weapon and will later find it unnecessary to fire it. However, as long as drawing the weapon is done as a means of advance preparation for the justifiable use of lethal force, the officer is showing good professional judgment in being prepared to take instant action should the occasion arise.

A common type of situation in which inexperienced officers have drawn their weapons is when they have stopped a car for a traffic violation. Recently, an off-duty officer forced a driver of a car that had nearly had a collision with his car to the side of the road. When the driver refused to get out of his auto, the officer pulled his revolver and ordered the man out. The driver still refused to leave his car, and while the officer was attempting to remove him forcibly, his revolver discharged and the citizen was wounded.

Although no criminal charges were filed against the officer, it was ruled that his actions had been excessive, and he was fired. A simple rule of thumb to determine whether he was justified in drawing his weapon under the existing circumstances is whether the citizen's refusal to get out of his car when ordered posed any immediate threat of bodily harm or death to the officer, and whether the officer would have been justified in shooting the citizen merely for failure to obey his orders.

Some officers feel justified in drawing their weapon as a means of re-enforcing their authority in situations where lethal force is not justified. The problem with this tactic is that some citizens feel equally strongly about not backing down before the officer's authority when they feel that the officer is wrong. In a confrontation of this type, the officer may feel compelled to carry out his threat of force or to back down. Unfortunately, in a few such incidents the officer has chosen unwisely to fire his weapon as the ultimate means of asserting his authority. The gravity of the taking of a human life cannot be overstated. Perhaps the soundest guideline for a police officer to use in deciding whether or not to fire his weapon is to ask himself whether the firing is necessary, unavoidable, and without any alternative. Taken as a whole, these three criteria constitute the reasonable cause that a police officer must have in order to justify his actions.

The authority to take a human life is a great responsibility. To assume this authority in a responsible way requires maturity, judgment, quick reflexes, and a thorough understanding of the law. In short, the person holding the legal authority of life and death must be a professional.

Warning Shots

Firing warning shots is as impractical in most cases as is shooting with intent to wound the suspect rather than to kill him. As stated earlier, the purpose of the weapon is to kill, and its purpose should not be broadened. Such an expansion of the purpose of the weapon would lead to increased questioning of the legality of killings by law enforcement officers. For example, if an officer were legally justified in firing his weapon as a warning to a suspect who was attempting to flee, and his warning shot struck and killed an innocent bystander, would the death of the bystander be justified or excusable because of the legality of firing warning shots? A warning shot will always end up by striking something. The risk that it will kill or injure some innocent person is not worth taking.

Some officers argue that warning shots sometimes serve to prevent the escape of a suspect who otherwise might have killed or injured others. This reasoning is weak. When an officer chooses to fire a warning shot, he usually does so because the suspect is already too far away for him to chase. In addition, the firing of the weapon, coupled with the fact that the suspect was not hit, is likely to urge the man to even greater efforts to escape.

The Night Stick

The police baton or nightstick usually ranges in length from twelve to twenty-four inches. In recent years many departments have begun converting almost entirely to the use of the longer weapon. Generally, the longer weapon is known as a riot stick and originally was used primarily in crowd control situations.

The reason for the increasing popularity among law enforcement personnel for the longer riot stick is its effectiveness as both an offensive and a defensive weapon. Properly handled and employed, the riot stick can be an extremely dangerous and even lethal weapon at short range. As a defensive weapon, it can be used to ward off kicks, blows, knife thrusts, and punches. As an offensive weapon, it can incapacitate, cripple, or kill.

The primary deficiency of the police baton, whether short or long, has not been in the weapon itself, but rather in the lack of expertise exhibited by police officers in its use. The maximum efficiency with which this weapon can be used has been developed into an art much like the Oriental methods of self-defense. It is a skill well worth learning and, like all skills, requires application and practice. A valuable book for any police officer interested in learning how to make maximum use of his baton has been written by Robert Koga, an officer with the Los Angeles Police Department. Koga's book is titled *The Koga Method: Police Weaponless Control & Defense Techniques* (Beverly Hills, Calif.: Glencoe Press, 1967). It is likely that once the effectiveness of this weapon becomes more fully recognized, many police departments will include it as a part of their recruit training program. Until that time, however, it would be to the individual officer's advantage to take it upon himself to become proficient in the Koga method of the use of the baton.

Recommended Reading

Gerald Leinwand, *The Police* (New York: Pocket Books, 1972).

CHAPTER 13

Recognizing and Handling Abnormal Persons

Police officers are frequently called upon to handle people who are mentally ill or addicted to alcohol or drugs. It is important to be able to recognize mental illness and to know what procedures to follow in dealing with violent and disturbed people.

Recognizing Mentally Ill Persons

Although it is not always easy to recognize that a person is mentally ill, there are certain signs that can provide clues. Some mentally ill persons may show all or most of these signs, and some may not show any of them. Most, however, will show at least one of the following:

Abrupt or drastic changes in behavior

Unexplained loss of memory
Behavior that is dangerous to himself or others
Complaints of bodily ailments that are not possible
Complaints of strange odors, peculiar tastes, or visions
A belief that people are plotting against him
A belief that people are continually watching him or talking about him
Talking to himself or claiming to hear voices

Usually the officer is not in a position to know whether the person's behavior has undergone an abrupt change. He will probably have to depend on the assessment of the person's relatives or friends. In questioning the subject, however, the officer can determine whether his thought processes are rational and whether he is fully aware of his surroundings. A simple test that can be used is similar to that used by coaches and managers of athletes. Particularly in boxing and football, when the athlete has suffered a hard blow, his coach or manager will ask him his name, his birth date, or the day of the week, or merely ask him where he is.

Some mentally ill persons are unable to comprehend that they can be injured by things that a normally alert person automatically avoids. A mentally ill person may hold a burning match in his hand until it actually burns his flesh. He may not be able to sense that water is too hot and that it will blister him. He may strike his fists against hard objects with such force that they break the skin or even break a bone.

All rules have exceptions, of course, and the guidelines for recognizing symptoms should not be considered applicable in all cases. While the claim that one hears voices is one of the accepted symptoms of mental disease, an example from a recent incident shows that there may be plausible exceptions. In one particular case a man in his mid-thirties, with no previous history of mental problems or serious medical problems, began complaining of hearing music and voices. The initial inclination of many persons close to him was to assume that he was undergoing stress from overwork and was on the verge of a nervous breakdown. Once when the man claimed to hear music he persuaded a friend to listen closely to see if he too could hear something. The friend did hear music, and the mystery was soon solved. The man had recently undergone extensive dental work that included fillings and metal braces. Through a freak, but not totally unknown, circumstance, the man's dental work was acting as a receiver of radio waves, and his dental work was picking up the transmissions from a local station.

All individuals without physical impairment have five physical senses. A mentally ill person may have hallucinations involving any of the senses. He may "hear" voices when no one is around, or he may claim to hear the voice of someone who is deceased. He may "see" something or someone when it is plainly impossible. Some mentally ill persons "feel" insects crawling on them, or claim to feel someone tapping them on the arm. Others "taste" poison in their food or "smell" strange odors. Many mentally ill persons who believe they smell foreign odors go to great lengths to seal doors and windows by stuffing newspapers around them and in keyholes of doors.

Some mentally ill persons believe that they are constantly being watched or talked about. This feeling may begin early in the illness, when the person is becoming sensitive because he feels that something is wrong with him. He begins to wonder whether others can see his problem, too, and he gradually begins to assume that whenever he sees two people talking they are talking about him. As his illness develops he becomes convinced that others are watching and talking about him.

Such a person may hear only part of a conversation as he passes some people on the street, and he may immediately assume that they are referring to him. While listening to the radio, he is likely to assume that any comments he hears are directed at him. If he hears his name mentioned, he is likely to be convinced beyond any doubt that he is the object of discussion.

A person who becomes upset by this type of occurrence is said to be affected by *ideas of reference.* Initially, these ideas of reference may occur only occasionally. Then they tend to gradually increase in frequency until they develop into easily observable delusions of persecution.

In most instances in which a police officer is called to investigate a person who is believed to be mentally ill, the individual will be in the first stages of the illness, and his symptoms, if visible at all, may be only slight. Typically, reports to the police of situations involving abnormal actions and suspected mental illness are made by husbands, wives, or grown children living with the affected person. It is well to remember that to the individual involved, these symptoms are very real, and his suffering from them can be as acute as if his illness were physical. In some instances individuals afflicted with a type of mental disorder live useful lives for years, and only those closest to them are aware of their problem. A former heavyweight boxer, known throughout the world, has had such an illness for years but is able to live a useful life because his illness is kept under control.

In more extreme cases the person afflicted can be a danger to himself, and it is the responsibility of the police officer called to the scene to determine whether the individual is likely to be a threat to himself or others. Once the officer has determined that the victim should be hospitalized for either his own protection or the protection of others, he should make every effort to persuade the husband, wife, or other close relative to arrange for such hospitalization.

Most jurisdictions have laws that allow the police officer, when no other means are available, to have the person suspected of mental illness committed immediately on his own authority. Usually, by use of either an ambulance or a patrol wagon, the individual is transported to the hospital for observation.

In one case of this type the officer had been called to a rooming house where tenants had reported that a young man was acting odd. They said that, while the person in question seemed normal most of the time, he became violently upset at the sound of an airplane; he would break into a sweat and attempt to hide under furniture or in closets to escape the noise.

The officer found out that the individual lived alone and that he had no close friends or relatives around who could take steps to have him committed. After questioning the man, the officer decided that he was in need of medical attention to keep him from harming himself. The officer was able to convince the young man that he needed help, and he offered no resistance when an ambulance was called to transport him to the hospital. At the hospital, however, the authorities did not place much stock in the officer's story and were on the verge of releasing the young man immediately. Fortunately, an airplane flew over at that moment, and it took several hospital attendants to restrain the young man from jumping out a window in his attempt to get away from the noise.

Handling Violent Persons

Fortunately, most mentally ill persons are neither violent nor dangerous. While they may be easily excitable and upset, their excitement usually lasts only a short time, and, if handled properly, they are usually quick to quiet down. The key to the proper handling of such a person is not to threaten or further frighten him.

When an officer is called upon to take a disturbed person into custody and the person is excited but not immediately dangerous, the officer should take his time and attempt to calm the subject down by being as low-key as possible. The disturbed person may view the officer's uniform as a badge of authority that is threatening to him. In order to calm the subject's fears, the officer many times can take his cap off and proceed in an informal manner. By apparently ignoring the subject's mannerisms, the officer can invite all parties to sit down and talk the situation over. Many times mentally ill persons are subconsciously looking for someone who can help them. If the officer is able to control the situation so that all persons present act in a calm, deliberate manner, it is likely that the disturbed person too will soon quiet down. Under no circumstances should the officer frighten the subject or threaten him. Although the disturbed person may not fully understand what the officer is attempting to do, if he senses that the officer is trying to help him, he will more than likely respond rationally.

Some mentally ill persons are quick to pick out weaknesses or points of irritation in others. They may ridicule a person for having large ears, protruding teeth, or other characteristics about which the person may be sensitive. The police officer must not let the disturbed person get under his skin. An experienced officer will recognize this tactic and will understand that it is an indication of a deep sense of inferiority and lack of self-confidence on the part of the subject. The person should be viewed as sick, confused, and frightened, and if at all possible should be approached with that in mind.

While the officer will not always be able to reason with a mentally ill person, if he remains both calm and firm the chances are better than even that the subject will begin to quiet down. Many disturbed persons are able to sense when someone is trying to help them, and when they recognize that the person means business they often start to cooperate. Even though some mentally ill persons will continue to fight and threaten, they still seem to recognize that the police officer represents a force stronger than themselves, and they therefore carry their protest only up to a certain point. In some situations they will abruptly drop their resistance and quietly do as they are told.

At this point it is doubly important that the officer not threaten the patient, not strike him, call him names, or try to bluff him. Such actions in all probability will only undo the progress that has been made and make the job harder and more dangerous.

If the individual fails to calm down and appears to the officer to be a threat to himself or others, the officer is justified in the use of force to subdue him. While the officer should be extremely careful not to use excessive force, he is not obligated to be injured himself before using necessary force on the patient. It is not necessary for a mentally ill person to have a prior history of such an illness, and, overall, mentally ill persons are unpredictable.

Recently, a young man in Maryland walked along the street shooting bystanders at random. He was finally killed by police officers, and while the subsequent investigation indicated that he had probably been ill for several years, there was no record to indicate that his illness had ever been treated.

Psychopathic Personalities

The police officer is likely to come in contact with more psychopathic personalities than is a person of almost any other occupation. Psychopathic persons are continually causing trouble for themselves or getting into trouble. It is important, therefore, for the police officer to have some guidelines for recognizing this type of person.

There are five general clues to look for in identifying psychopathic personalities:

1. They tend to provoke trouble.

2. They exercise little if any self-control.

3. They lack the kind of conscience that tells them whether some act is good or bad. Their judgment is warped or lacking.

4. They do not seem to learn by experience.

5. When they want something, they are unwilling to wait until an appropriate time for it.

Basically, these clues define what is commonly termed a character defect. An interesting aspect of persons who have this type of disorder is that in many cases they have a certain charm and appear to be bright and articulate. Not all such persons have outward symptoms that would lead to their identification as mentally ill.

Many such persons are successfully employed in occupations in which they meet and deal with the public, particularly in sales work. They tend to be glib, but also tend to be untruthful and lack remorse over having lied to someone. They are also unreliable. A psychopathic person is generally judged to be shallow in his feelings toward others, with no capacity to love anyone else. He thinks in terms of himself and how his actions will affect him personally. With these characteristics, it is easy to see how such persons would become involved in "get-rich-quick" schemes and go into business ventures that border on the criminal.

Above all, such a person is unable to recognize that there is something wrong with him. No matter how outlandish the situation, he is able to find the other person at fault in all his problems. Some such persons are prone to threaten suicide without much thought behind the threat and seldom with any intent to carry it out.

Except in extreme cases a psychopath is deemed under criminal laws as being responsible for his acts, and he is punished rather than treated. The police officer who must deal with a psychopathic person should always keep in mind that such a person, while seeming to be very sincere, is in fact a shallow person who is capable of blaming the officer for his predicament. Such a person is unlikely to display nervousness in the presence of an officer and should be watched very closely and not given an opportunity to catch the officer at a disadvantage.

Alcoholism and Drug Addiction

Statistics indicate that in the matter of arrests, the police officer deals with persons under the influence of alcohol more often than any other type of offender. There is a difference, however, between a person who is merely drunk and a person who is an alcoholic. Specifically, the alcoholic is addicted to the excessive use of liquor.

Alcoholism has now become recognized as a disease to be treated, and not as a crime to be punished. It is still a practice in many jurisdictions, however, to lump all persons who are drunk into the same category and to prosecute them criminally. The individual officer on the street is not able to set policy in matters of this type and must follow the dictates of his department in handling such matters.

Drunkenness itself is usually not too difficult a problem for the police officer to handle. A determination of how the drunk individual should be handled is based in part on the situation in which the officer came in contact with him. If the individual is with friends who can care for him or is in his own home, it often is better for the officer to take no official action. It is when the person is a potential hazard to himself or to others that the officer is obligated to take action. The specific action that the officer takes will in most cases be based on his own experience in spotting the underlying problem.

One rather common condition that the officer will be called upon to handle involves the person with the D.T.'s (delirium tremens). This condition is also referred to as "the shakes." A person suffering the D.T.'s is an individual who has been drinking for years and has become overly fatigued, or has not been eating, or has been suddenly cut off from his supply of alcohol.

Under these conditions the person becomes delirious and confused as to his surroundings and may begin to have hallucinations. His whole body may start shaking uncontrollably. Such a person is in need of immediate medical attention. It is still not totally unheard of for individuals with this condition to be thrown in jail "to sleep it off." It also is not unheard of for such persons to die in jail.

A somewhat similar condition, whose victims do not exhibit

the marked degree of abnormality as do persons with the D.T.'s is acute hallucinosis. This is found in persons who have been drinking heavily for a long period of time. They begin to "see" and "hear" things, but at the same time they are perfectly aware of everything that is going on around them. Individuals with these symptoms do not have the shakes. This condition will last longer than will the D.T.'s.

A person exhibiting either of these symptoms is ill, and it is the police officer's responsibility to help him the same as he would any sick person. Just as one reason for arresting a drunk on the street is to protect him while he is defenseless, a person with the D.T.'s is in need of protection in the form of hospitalization.

The drug problem in this country has become increasingly complex over the past decade. Laws governing the possession, use, and sale of drugs have also changed drastically. For the most part, only officers who specialize in the investigation of drug-related offenses are thoroughly knowledgeable of the various types and appearances of the many illegal drugs.

This is not to say, however, that the patrol officer need not have any specialized knowledge of drugs. In order to carry out his duties professionally, the patrol officer should have a good basic understanding of this problem and be able to spot the symptoms of drug addiction.

Three terms that are regularly used when referring to persons who use drugs are *habituation, tolerance,* and *addiction. Habituation* refers to the tendency of the user to become mentally dependent on the drug so that he believes he cannot get along without it. From a physical standpoint, however, such a person does not suffer any ill effects from discontinuing the use of the drug. *Tolerance* is the body's resistance to a drug. As the body builds up endurance, larger and larger amounts of the drug must be taken in order to produce the same mental or physical result as was attained when the individual first started using the drug. *Addiction* is physical dependence upon the drug to the extent that the user can become physically ill—and in some cases even die—without its continued use.

It is at the point of addiction that users are most likely to become criminals. Because of the larger and larger quantities of the drug that he must have in order to keep going, the addict must use any means available to support his habit. He is forced by his condition to become a liar, even to his own family and his closest friends. He becomes untrustworthy and unreliable and eventually loses his own self-respect, all because of his great need for the drug. Obviously, such a person can exhibit unpredictable behavior. A police officer cannot become careless when dealing with a person he knows is an addict, or a person who, because of his symptoms, the officer suspects is an addict. If an addict believes he is about to be arrested, and therefore deprived of his drug, he may go to great lengths to prevent his arrest. While it is generally true that the drug addict is not prone to violence, his addiction makes him a potentially dangerous person.

The symptoms that identify a drug addict are many and varied. Most common are a runny nose, watery eyes, sniffling, and a tendency to slouch or bend over as if it is painful to stand erect. An addict who has recently had a heroin "fix" has a tendency to be extremely relaxed and even appear sleepy. He is, in effect, "coasting," or under the influence of the drug. Such persons are generally not violent, but when they do become violent they seem to have a reserve of strength to draw on, and because of a temporary high pain tolerance, they are difficult to subdue.

Several manuals that deal with methods recommended for police officers to use in handling drug addicts remind the officer that the drug addict, like the alcoholic, is mentally and physically sick and that the officer should attempt to protect him. Such advice is not realistic, however. Admittedly, the addict is sick. But when he chooses to resist a police officer he does so because he believes he must maintain his freedom in order to continue his illegal habit. Such a person is very likely to use whatever means is necessary and available in order to obtain his freedom. The police officer should at all times be prepared to protect himself.

The drug addict is unreliable and unpredictable. The time to treat him as a sick person is after he is safely in custody, not when the officer is attempting to take him into custody.

Sex Offenders

Sex offenses include a wide range of criminal acts; from forcible rape to female impersonation. Generally, a sex offender is considered to be anyone who violates a criminal law relating to sexual behavior. Just as the acts have a wide range, the individuals who commit these acts can vary from persons who would otherwise be judged normal to those who have been adjudged sexual psychopaths.

The most common types of sexual offenses with which the patrol officer is called upon to deal are rape, homosexuality, indecent exposure (exhibitionism), and voyeurism ("peeping Toms").

The general view held by psychiatrists is that a person who commits a serious sexual crime is usually mentally ill. Many such persons have given no previous indication of such an illness and are married and well respected in their community. Such individuals may be having their first official contact with a police officer and are understandably extremely fearful of the possible public exposure and embarrassment that may follow their arrest.

In most instances, persons who have been involved in an illegal sexual offense are not likely to be violent when accosted by a police officer. There are exceptions, of course, particularly if the person greatly fears public exposure and feels that it is absolutely necessary for him to evade arrest.

When questioning suspects in connection with sex offenses, the officer should be particularly careful not to degrade or insult the suspect. The primary purpose of questioning is to learn just what the suspect did and then to gain an admission from him. If the suspect feels that he is being ridiculed or demeaned, it is very unlikely that he will in any way be cooperative in an interview. In this type of interview or interrogation, a skilled officer will appear to sympathize with the suspect's predicament, thereby making it easier for the suspect to discuss what occurred. This can be done by softening the language in questioning the suspect. As an example, rather than asking a suspect bluntly if he raped the complainant, the officer can lead up to this question by getting the suspect to discuss how and when he came in contact with the woman, whether she encouraged him, and finally, instead of asking "Did you rape her?" he can ask "Did you have intercourse with her?" While an admission of intercourse does not constitute rape, in all probability if the suspect was bluntly asked if he had raped the victim, he would have answered "No." Once he has admitted that a sexual act did take place, he is in the position of explaining the circumstances surrounding the act. If the victim had been beaten, or had been attacked in the street, it is unlikely that the suspect could concoct a story that would reasonably explain away the fact.

The same tactic is useful with exhibitionists and "peeping Toms." With the sympathetic approach, it is usually not too difficult to get the suspect to make some degree of admission while he is attempting to justify his predicament. With exhibitionism, for example, many suspects who have been accused of exposing themselves to women will claim that they didn't realize that their pants were open, or that they had to urinate and didn't realize that anyone saw them. In one case the suspect was in the habit of standing naked in his garage and opening the door just as a woman would walk by. The man claimed that it was his habit to exercise in his garage, and that he was actually wearing skin-colored tights. If the officer had bluntly accused the suspect of being an exhibitionist, it is likely that the man would have flatly denied the entire allegation. As it was, because he felt that the officer would believe him, he chose to fabricate a story that explained why the woman thought she observed him naked. However, once the suspect admitted that the woman did see him in the garage, he was asked to produce his flesh-colored tights. He was unable to do so.

Another problem with which the patrol officer is likely to have to deal involves interviews with parents of teen-age boys suspected of sex offenses. Sex offenses by teen-agers often involve "peeping" or sexual relations with girls under the legal age of consent, also called statutory rape. Surprising as it may seem, a great many parents, regardless of the weight of evidence shown them, will refuse to believe that their son could be guilty of a sex offense. Many of these parents are actually more concerned with their own personal embarrassment within their community, but whatever their reasoning, they are likely to lie deliberately to the officer in an attempt to protect their son. This can pose a difficult situation, because in some such cases there is simply insufficient evidence on which to base an arrest without cooperation from either the suspect or his parents.

One possible way of handling this type of situation is to talk to the parents separately. In some cases a father will be more understanding of the problems that a teen-age boy can get into and, if given the opportunity to discuss the case with the officer out of the presence of his wife, will be more reasonable and more cooperative. Generally, a mother is simply not capable of admitting or believing that her son could be involved in an illegal sex act, particularly if she is raising a son without a husband in the home. Many such women feel defensive, as if it is a reflection on them as a mother if their son is guilty of such crimes.

In some investigations involving sex crimes it is possible for the officer to talk to the youthful suspect out of the presence of either his mother or father. This situation gives the officer the best opportunity to develop the facts of the case. Many boys, although they might not be particularly embarrassed to admit a sex offense, would be unable to make any such admission in the presence of their parents. An experienced officer can take advantage of this type of situation by convincing the suspect that the officer will explain the whole matter to the boy's parents in such a manner that they will not be shocked or offended. Many young suspects in this position are sincerely looking for help and for a sympathetic person to talk to. Often they simply do not feel that they can discuss sexual problems with their parents, so when they do get into trouble, they are likely to seek someone who will explain their problems to their parents for them.

Since the majority of persons who come in contact with the police for sex offenses are first offenders—at least insofar as being caught is concerned—they are likely to be very afraid and to be seeking someone who will give them advice and sympathize with them. An officer who treats such a suspect in a skillful, yet sympathetic, manner is far more likely to gain the truth from the suspect than is the officer who curses or degrades the suspect.

The officer must make judgments based on the evidence available to him at the time whether an individual is mentally ill, under the influence of liquor, or possibly under the influence of drugs. On more than a few occasions individuals have been arrested for drunkenness, and later—sometimes too late—it was discovered that the person was a diabetic and was entering diabetic shock.

While there is no way to insure that the officer will never make such a mistake in judgment, the possibility can be minimized by his being aware of the general symptoms for the suspected problem and his reluctance to take the word of witnesses without personally checking on the individual's condition and symptoms.

When the officer determines to take a course of action based on his assessment of the situation but still has reservations as to the individual's problem, he should make sure to note his observations and reservations on the report that he submits with the subject when he is transported to the hospital or jail. In this way he makes sure that his reservations will be a matter of record, and at the same time he alerts hospital or jail authorities to assess further the individual's condition.

Recommended Reading

Theodore R. Sarbin, ed., *Studies in Behavior Pathology* (New York: Holt, Rinehart and Winston, 1962).

CHAPTER 14

Community
Relations

The purpose of police community relations is to strive, through
a planned program, to build community confidence in and understanding of the role of the police department and its objectives.
A department should continually aim to advance this relationship between the police and individuals and groups in the community. In order to attain these aims, cooperation and
communication between the citizenry and the department must
be promoted continually by building public confidence in the
department and by gaining support for departmental objectives,
including compliance with laws, assistance in investigations, and
endorsement of special police programs.

Community Relations versus Public Relations

In practice, police tend to confuse community relations with
public relations. In part because of their feelings of isolation, they

tend to try to "sell" the community on their role and their practices. This usually involves various types of presentations by the department in which its best image is projected. While public relations should be a function of the department, it should not be confused with, or combined with, community relations. A community relations program that is to be workable and beneficial must have a mechanism for an interchange of suggestions, views, and criticisms between the department and individuals or groups.

Some departments have attempted to screen out this valuable source of community input by choosing not to cooperate with groups that have been critical of them or groups whose political philosophy differs from that which is represented by the majority of the department's officers. This tactic makes the theoretical role of community relations self-defeating. It is much more likely that the frictions and misunderstandings between the department and some segment of the community will be brought out into the open if meaningful communications are maintained with the groups who voice criticisms.

It should constantly be remembered that a successful community relations operation makes the department's job of law enforcement and criminal investigation much easier.

Objectives

It is not enough for a department to have a few officers designated as "community relations officers," whose primary purpose is to promote the relationship between the department and the community, if the image that these officers project is not reflected by the rest of the department. Too often, usually in large departments, the community relations section is viewed by the rest of the department with resentment or disdain. Many officers, particularly older ones, feel that this unit gives the impression that the department is going soft or is weak in law and order.

It is precisely because of this attitude that the major problem in community relations has been the department itself rather than the community. Over the past decade citizen complaints and criticisms of the police have increased drastically, primarily in the areas of discrimination against minorities, unnecessary physical and verbal abuse, and authoritarian attitudes that make them unable to deal justly with citizens. Again, the overall attitude exhibited by the police has caused them to be identified as feeling insecure in their role and has contributed to their inability to deal openly and objectively with such complaints and criticisms.

It has become increasingly apparent that in some instances the police are corrupt, brutal, and authoritarian. Such behavior is bound to occur to some extent in any large military or semimilitary organization, and the greatest disservice that the organization can do is to deny its existence. The overall objective therefore becomes one of actively seeking the community's cooperation and assistance in upgrading not only the quality of the department's officers but also the quality of service the department gives the community. An accurate and up-to-date evaluation of either of these factors can be obtained only if there is meaningful two-way communication between the department and the total community.

The Need for Community Backing

As stated earlier, a department's success in its law enforcement role is tied to its relationship with the community. Other areas, too, are dependent on the police-community relationship. There are many fringe benefits available to police officers that hinge, at least in part, on the relationship between the department and the community. Working conditions, salary, insurance, retirement benefits, and educational incentives are only a few of the areas that can be achieved much more easily—or only—with the support of the community.

The animosity and resentment toward the police that has resulted from too many unresolved abrasive incidents need not exist. If the community believes in its police department, there is no need for the authoritarian attitude that some departments adopt. Problems can be dealt with on both sides as individual incidents or acts, rather than as an overall attitude or philosophy exhibited by the department. An additional factor that tends to work to the advantage of the individual police officer accused of misbehavior is that if the department as a whole has a good reputation in the community, there is less pressure for drastic action to be taken against an officer found in violation of a department regulation or to have acted improperly in his dealings with a citizen.

Prejudice and Race Relations

The President's Commission on Law Enforcement and Administration of Justice stated in its report *The Challenge of Crime in a Free Society,* "The commission believes that a police-community relations program is one of the most important functions of any police department in a community with a substantial minority population." The grievances that blacks have expressed against the police are not without basis. They have experienced neglect and discrimination and have generally been accorded a second-class status insofar as their overall treatment has been concerned. Over a period of time these grievances have led to a smoldering resentment toward *all* authority. As a visible symbol of authority, the police have borne the brunt of outbursts of hostile actions and resentments generated by years of discrimination. Unfortunately, in too many instances the police have responded to these hostile actions or attitudes by overreacting, thereby compounding the problem.

After several summers that were highlighted by major riots and police-citizen confrontations that ended in violence and in some cases death, the widespread violence has dwindled to occasional outbursts. Gone are the major riots such as Watts, Newark, Washington, D.C., and Detroit. It is no mere coincidence that these forms of violence subsided at the same time that police departments adopted a more enlightened approach to their problems with the communities they served. In more and more cities, minority groups have found a mechanism within the police department for dealing with their complaints. In these cities a restoration of public confidence in the police has taken place. This change in attitude has been brought about by action rather than rhetoric.

Gradually more and more police officers have come to recognize the importance of building a better rapport with citizens of all races and classes. While this attitude runs counter to the old-line established view that the officer must maintain the stern, distant, stereotyped image of the "tough cop," its value as a means of assisting the officer in doing his job is becoming increasingly evident. Riots have shown that the police cannot possibly maintain order if a majority of the citizens are not law-abiding. Therefore, respect for police officers encourages respect for the laws he is charged with enforcing. This respect is not automatic, however; it must be earned.

Since there are few occasions when an officer actually witnesses an offense being committed, he must rely on the cooperation of citizens of all races and classes to assist him in doing his job. The quickest way to forfeit that assistance is to exhibit prejudice. .

It does not necessarily follow that community relations in a police department should be confined to a separate section or unit. Experience has shown that, particularly in smaller departments, while one or two men should be assigned to organizing and scheduling various types of meetings and discussions with citizen groups, the job of making police community relations work belongs to the entire department. The best way to make this approach productive is to have regularly scheduled meetings within the department so that all the officers can be brought up to date on various types of community problems or complaints. Such meetings can also be used to point out the department's shortcomings and the errors that it may have made in dealing with specific community problems. In short, the most effective way to enable an officer to deal with either individuals or groups in problems related to police-community relations is to make him knowledgeable of those problems and of the alternative methods by which they can be solved.

The individual patrol officer should guard against a tendency to view himself as working in an alien community and should take particular care to guard against such an attitude in his relationships with the citizens he comes in contact with. It has been noted that the relationship between a police officer and a person he comes in contact with in the line of duty is always unequal. This inequality is a major factor in limiting the degree of cooperation the officer can realistically expect from the citizen. This feeling of inequality need not exist, however, and the officer who has succeeded in developing a relationship with persons on his beat that is based on mutual respect rather than on subconscious fear of his authority is much more likely to receive both assistance and information he may need.

Areas of particular sensitivity include the use of profanity, overfamiliarity, and the quirks of each officer's individual personality. It has been found that an officer's use of profanity is sometimes viewed as an indication of his feeling that he has a right to "privileged familiarity" in dealing with persons he views as of lower class than himself. Overfamiliarity usually takes the form of the officer's addressing persons by their first names while assuming that he should be addressed by his title or by his last name. This habit is particularly grating to blacks, many of whom came from the southern part of the United States where they were routinely insulted by whites who addressed them as "boy" or by their first names.

Perhaps one of the most difficult problems for the individual officer, particularly a new officer, in developing a good working relationship with citizens involves his own personality. Because of their view of what a professional police officer should be, some young officers tend to adopt an impersonal attitude in dealing with citizens instead of trying to fit their own individual personalities into the demands of the profession. As an example, if an officer is naturally friendly and interested in people, he should not suppress his natural traits merely to conform to what he views as the restrictions placed on him by his profession. Friendliness and curiosity can be valuable to a police officer. An officer who is viewed as friendly is much better able to learn information important to him through seemingly innocent and natural conversations than is the officer who projects a "professional" attitude to the extent that anytime he converses with a citizen, the person feels he is being interrogated or is under suspicion.

All these factors involve police-community relations. They are important not only for the image of the department that they help project but even more as a tool for more efficient law enforcement.

Over the past few years it has become increasingly apparent that the problem of crime is not solely the responsibility of the police, but that its prevention depends to a great degree on community cooperation. It is because of this need for community cooperation that police departments have begun stepping up their efforts to educate citizens about crime and how to prevent it and protect themselves.

Recently the Dallas (Texas) police department instituted a program in which methods of crime prevention have been shown on television in professional productions. Community awareness and willingness to become involved can greatly decrease crime and increase the effectiveness of the police. One chief of police recently stated that if citizens would just *close* their garage doors, not even lock them, burglaries in that city would be decreased by 10 percent.

More than ever before, police are in the public eye. We have shifted to a predominately urban society, with populations concentrated in cities that are increasingly difficult to police. These population concentrations have brought about social change, and the police will have to respond and change themselves to keep pace with these changes. The police cannot afford to be apart from the community. To be effective, to do the job they are intended to do, they must be a part of the community, responsible and responsive.

Recommended Reading

Louis A. Radelet, *The Police and the Community* (Beverly Hills: Glencoe Press, 1973).

CHAPTER 15

Conclusion: Necessary Qualities for the Successful Police Officer

While it may seem that the prerequisites for a successful police officer should be examined at the beginning of a book of this kind, there is a particular reason for dealing with them in conclusion. The examination of the patrol officer's various roles and methods of operation should help the individual officer to be more aware of his position and his responsibilities.

Once the officer has gained sufficient knowledge or proper operational procedures and is able to put his knowledge into practice, he should continually assess his own performance in order to evaluate his improvement and his increased professionalism. There is no doubt that there should be continued improvement. An officer who is interested in his job, in serving the community to the best of his ability, and in performing in a professional manner is bound to increase his professionalism if he continually analyzes his actions in previous incidents.

Many skills that the officer gains with experience can only be developed by repeated exposure in actual situations. No amount of practice in interrogation can be as valuable as the real thing. Most rookie officers either overstep their abilities the first few times they undertake the task of interrogating a suspect, or they exhibit their lack of experience to the extent that the suspect is able to take advantage of them. It is in just such an area as this that the sincerely dedicated officer can evaluate his own performance and identify his shortcomings.

Too often the police tend to become overly concerned with their image and with an exaggerated concept of their role. In some instances police officers gradually adopt the position that they have the responsibility for deciding what is good for the general public and for punishing suspected offenders.

Recently I talked with a young woman who explained that she had been very negative in her feelings about the police and extremely suspicious of their motives. She arranged to take part in a "ride-along" program in the city in which she lived and was able to observe first-hand the actions and attitudes of several officers. She described how the scout car in which she was riding responded, along with several other cars, to a call to a local bar where a man suspected of being a child molester was said to have been spotted. When the car arrived at the scene, other officers were already bringing the suspect out of the bar. Several officers were beating the suspect, who was not resisting. The officer with whom the woman was riding explained to her that most of the officers involved in the beating were family men who were justifiably upset with a man suspected of molesting small children. The woman stated that this incident changed her whole perspective of the police, and that she learned from that experience to sympathize with them and with the problems they faced.

Were the officers justified in their attitudes? Were they justified in their actions of beating the suspect? Should the woman have felt they were justified? Up to the point at which the suspect was taken into custody, there was no proof that he had committed a crime. The information available to the officers was that a man was suspected of being a child molester.

Suppose the man they took into custody was not the person referred to as the suspect? Suppose he was the right suspect, but was not guilty of any crime? Suppose he was guilty? Under any of these circumstances would the officers have been justified in beating him? The responsibility of the police is not to punish; it is to prevent crime and to protect life and property. In this case the responsibility of the police was to take the suspect into custody and to protect him, not to punish him for something they believed he might have done.

In a somewhat similar situation a San Francisco police officer stopped a middle-aged black man who had been pointed out to him by a teen-age black girl. The girl claimed that a few hours earlier the man had forcibly raped her. The officer took the man into custody and in the process severely beat the man about the head with his night stick. The man was so badly injured that he required plastic surgery.

It required only a preliminary investigation to determine that (1) the young girl had not been raped, (2) she was mentally deficient, and (3) the man she accused of raping her was at work at the time the alleged offense was supposed to have taken place. The officer lost his job, was charged with felony assault, and was convicted. Character testimony at the officer's trial indicated that basically he was a very gentle person who was known to shy away from violence. Why then would he assault a middle-aged man who was neither resisting his arrest nor attempting to escape? The answer probably lies in peer group pressure. The officer had probably subconsciously absorbed the attitudes of some of the older officers and had come to believe that his role was to mete out punishment when he believed it was justified and necessary. In believing the girl's story, he simply forgot the concept that a man is considered innocent until proven guilty, and he decided at the scene that the suspect was guilty.

In addition to deciding the suspect's guilt, he "sentenced" the suspect to corporal punishment. One might hope that this was the first time that particular officer put "street justice" into practice, but the fact that he so openly and severely beat the suspect might indicate that he was a veteran at this type of law enforcement.

A police officer must keep an open mind in order to do a fair and effective job. His duties bring him into contact with all types of individuals in all types of situations. It has been said many times that the police officer usually sees the citizen at his worst. The police, because of their role, deal with people under stress, people who are often in a state of shock or who are under some type of pressure that causes them to lie, bluster, beg, or in some way humiliate themselves. This does not mean, however, that these persons are deserving of any less respect from the officer than he has a right to expect from them.

In his book, *Violence and the Police*, author William A. West-ley has a chapter entitled "The Public as Enemy." Westley exam-ines the many ways in which police officers—and police departments—attempt to justify various types of disrespect and brutality that they direct toward citizens. He stresses the point that, to the police, it is all important that they stick together in order to protect each other against allegations of misconduct. All experienced police officers are familiar with the term "the blue coat code of silence." The code of silence stresses that each officer's loyalty should be to all other officers over and above their oath to uphold the law.

In the last ten years, however, a different type of young officer has been attracted to a police career, and it has been encouraging to see that many of them simply have not accepted the time-honored concept of loyalty to their brother officer even if he is wrong. This new attitude has begun to filter to the top command levels in many departments, and in the last few years it has been responsible for a decided change in both policy and practice in some departments. Inherent in the new concept is the attitude that being a police officer is belonging to a profession, and profes-sionals have standards that they are obligated to meet.

Race prejudice has been one of the most sensitive areas for the police to deal with effectively. All of us, in varying degrees, have some type of prejudice. In one sense a person suffers no harm simply because others are prejudiced against him. The attitude becomes harmful, however, when the prejudiced person uses his position or authority to put his attitude into practice. The white police officer who addresses a black man as "boy" is effectively insulting the man. Because of the officer's authority, however, the black man may not respond in such a way as to let the officer know of his deep-seated resentment at being called "boy." More important, on a long-term basis, is the hate and disrespect that the black man will direct toward that particular officer, and very likely toward all police officers.

In some instances racial prejudice is not a department-wide problem, but rather is reflected in the attitudes and practices of relatively few officers. This is the easier type of prejudice to counter. It is not necessary to make an officer change his life-long feelings. It is necessary only to impress upon him the standard of conduct that will be demanded of him in the performance of his duties.

Institutional prejudice, where negative attitudes and practices based on race are a reflection of the command structure of a department, usually indicates a lack of communication of near-crisis proportions between that department and a segment of the community it serves.

An example of institutional racism or prejudice in practice was shown a few years ago in a West Coast police department. In the early 1960's the department recruited its first Chinese officer. The new officer was a college graduate, with a B.S. degree in criminalistics. His academic background plainly indicated that he was highly qualified to conduct scientific investigations in the police crime laboratory. Rather than assigning him to this important and responsible position, however, the department assigned the young officer to beat patrol, where he remained for over three years.

During this time he developed into a very good police officer, able to handle himself well in any type of situation with which he was called upon to deal. The Chinese officer then took and passed the promotional examination for sergeant, and the department was faced with an institutional problem. The command structure within the department simply could not conceive of a Chinese officer in a command position. The "problem" had also been the subject of discussion among many of the officers who would have been under the Chinese officer's command, and they had made their dissatisfaction with the prospect known to their superiors.

The department finally "solved" the "problem" by taking an action that they could have taken three years earlier. They assigned the new sergeant to the crime laboratory. The problem to be recognized here is that the institutional prejudice within the department caused the original problem and then magnified the problem when the Chinese officer earned a promotion. If that particular department retains its racial attitudes, how is it likely to respond if the Chinese officer is promoted to lieutenant or captain?

On its face, the idea that an individual officer's attitude would have any impact on the policies or practices of a department as a whole may seem remote. History has already shown, however, that many "individual" officers have already brought about much-needed changes in police practices. Good common sense and values simply do not go out of style. In some situations they are suppressed for selfish motives, but in the end, the same attitudes that were suppressed are the ones that are needed to straighten out a bad situation.

The *Report of the National Advisory Commission on Civil Disorders* noted that ". . . Negroes firmly believe that police brutality and harrassment occur repeatedly in Negro neighborhoods."[1] The question of whether police brutality does in fact occur is no longer seriously debated. Instead, we attempt to minimize its seriousness by stressing the number of police-citizen contacts in which such illegal actions do not take place.

Some officers feel justified in treating certain individuals or groups with less respect, or with more harshness, than they would members of their own race or group. Surveys have indicated that an appreciable number of police officers admit anti-Negro feelings, view the Negro as biologically inferior, naturally lazy and irresponsible, "still savages," and other similar negative assessments.[2] As was pointed out earlier, it is when these biases or prejudices are put into action that charges of racism and brutality are leveled against the police in general.

Social control and peer pressure are not just theoretical concepts when applied to the new police officer; they are facts of life. The new officer is continually under stress from older, more experienced officers to reject any formal education he has received relative to the job and to accept the older officers' advice based on experience. From his veteran partner, the rookie officer is expected to learn the "right" way to act and to deal with different situations. He is taught not to be too "soft" with people, not to take any "stuff" off anybody, and above all, "everybody hates a cop. . . . You gotta make them respect you."[3]

It is difficult not to accept the teachings of one's peers when the "teacher" has the advantage of years of experience on the job. However, these teachings, when they are based on race prejudice, class prejudice, rumor, fiction, and ego reinforcement, are not merely worthless; they are potentially harmful to the new officer. The West Coast police officer who beat the man he suspected of raping the teen-age girl may have been acting out of his own beliefs that the supect represented a race that was morally deficient. Similarly, the officer may have believed that the courts were lax and that it was his responsibility to insure that the "guilty" man was punished. In either situation the officer would have been operating from a false base that in the end not only warped his logic but caused him to be convicted as a criminal.

To be a successful police officer is to recognize that the officer's role is to serve the public. To become increasingly skillful in serving the public the officer should recognize that every day on the job is part of a continuing learning process.

The effectiveness of any law enforcement agency depends on the amount of public support and cooperation it receives. The individual officer is the law, and therefore the effectiveness of his role is even more personally dependent on support and cooperation.

Recommended Reading

David Durk, "Viva La Policia," in *Law and Order: The Scales of Justice*, edited by Abraham S. Blumberg (New Brunswick, N.J.: Transaction Books, 1973).

Notes

CHAPTER 1   THE DEMAND FOR COMPETENCE

1. President's Commission on Law Enforcement and Administration of Justice, *Task Force Report: The Police* (Washington, D.C.: U.S. Government Printing Office, 1967), p. 1.

2. Ibid., p. 37.

3. Ibid., p. 116.

4. California Department of Justice, Bureau of Criminal Statistics, *Criminal Justice Agency Resources in California*, 1971, p. 11.

5. George H. Brereton, "The Importance of Training in the Progression of Law Enforcement," *Journal of Criminal Law, Criminology, and Police Science* 52 (1961).

6. Gerald Leinwand, ed., *The Police* (New York: Pocket Books, 1972), p. 58.

CHAPTER 3 ROUTINE PATROL PRACTICES

1. From the *Law Enforcement Code of Ethics.*

CHAPTER 5 REPORTS AND THE POLICE NOTEBOOK

1. Charles E. O'Hara, *Fundamentals of Criminal Investigation* (Springfield, Ill.: Charles E. Thomas, 1967), p. 43.

CHAPTER 9 SPECIFIC TACTICS AND TEAMWORK

1. Ramsey Clark, *Crime in America* (New York: Pocket Books, 1971), p. 123.

CHAPTER 15 CONCLUSION: NECESSARY QUALITIES FOR THE SUCCESSFUL POLICE OFFICER

1. U.S. Riot Commission, *Report of the National Advisory Commission on Civil Disorders* (Washington, D.C.: U.S. Government Printing Office, 1968).
2. William A. Westley, *Violence and the Police* (Cambridge, Mass.: Massachusetts Institute of Technology Press, 1970), p. 100.
3. Ibid., p. 159.

Bibliography

Blumberg, Abraham S., ed. *Law and Order: The Scales of Justice*. New Brunswick, N.J.: Transaction Books, 1973.

Creamer, J. Shane. *The Law of Arrest, Search and Seizure*. Philadelphia: W. B. Saunders, 1968.

Denfield, Duane. *Streetwise Criminology*. Cambridge, Mass.: Schenkman, 1974.

Ferdico, John N. *Criminal Procedure for the Law Enforcement Officer*. St. Paul, Minn.: West, 1975.

Mathews, Robert A., M.D., and Rayland, Lloyd, M.D. *How to Recognize and Handle Abnormal People*. New York, N.Y.: National Association for Mental Health, 1954.

Mitford, Jessica. *Kind and Usual Punishment*. New York: Alfred A. Knopf, 1973.

Niederhoffer, Arthur. *Behind the Shield*. New York: Doubleday, 1967.

O'Connor, George W., and Vanderbosch, Charles G. *The Patrol Operation*. Washington, D.C.: International Association of Chiefs of Police, 1967.

President's Commission on Law Enforcement and Administration of Justice.

The Challenge of Crime in a Free Society. Washington, D.C.: U.S. Government Printing Office, 1967.

————. *Task Force Report: The Police.* Washington, D.C.: U.S. Government Printing Office, 1967.

Quinney, Richard, ed. *Criminal Justice in America.* Boston, Mass.: Little, Brown, 1974.

Report of the National Advisory Commission on Civil Disorders, Otto Kerner, Chairman. Washington, D.C.: U.S. Government Printing Office, 1968.

Staff Report to the National Commission on the Causes and Prevention of Violence. *Law and Order Reconsidered.* Washington, D.C.: U.S. Government Printing Office, 1969.

State of California Department of Justice. *The Mentally Disordered Sex Offender.* Sacramento, Calif.: Bureau of Criminal Statistics, 1972.

Trojanowicz, Robert C., Trojanowicz, John M., and Moss, Forrest M. *Community Based Crime Prevention.* Pacific Palisades, Calif.: Goodyear, 1975.

Uviller, H. Richard. *The Processes of Criminal Justice: Investigation.* St. Paul, Minn.: West, 1974.

Ward, Richard H. *Introduction to Criminal Investigation.* Reading, Mass.: Addison-Wesley, 1975.

Westley, William A. *Violence and the Police.* Cambridge, Mass.: Massachusetts Institute of Technology Press, 1970.

Whisenand, Paul M., Cline, James L., and Felkenes, George T. *Police-Community Relations.* Pacific Palisades, Calif.: Goodyear, 1974.

Wilkins, Roy, and Clark, Ramsey. *Search and Destroy.* New York: Metropolitan Applied Research Center, Inc., 1973.

Index

About the Author

Gwynne Walker Peirson is that rare individual who has had a successful career as a police officer and now is into his second career as a college teacher.

He joined the Oakland, California, police department in 1947 after war-time service with the U.S. Air Corps as a captain with seventy combat missions as a fighter pilot. For eleven years he was a homicide investigator with the Oakland department. In 1970 he was elected as the first president of the Oakland, California, Black Officers Association.

On retiring from the department in 1970, he went to the University of Missouri as a lecturer and training director of security guards in housing projects in St. Louis. He has been a consultant for the Alameda (California) Regional Criminal Justice Planning Board, the U.S. Department of Justice Community Relations Service, and the University of Maryland.

After retiring from the force, Peirson returned to school and acquired his master's degree in criminology in 1971 from the University of California, where he is continuing work on his doctorate. He acquired his AA degree and his bachelor's while working full-time as a police officer.

He currently is a lecturer in the department of sociology and anthropology at Howard University.